# A History of Wednesbury in the County of Stafford [By J.N. Bagnall]

THE PARISH CHURCH OF WEDNESBURY PREVIOUS TO THE ALTERATIONS.

A

# HISTORY OF WEDNESBURY,

IN THE

## County of Stafford.

COMPILED

FROM VARIOUS AUTHENTIC SOURCES, BOTH ANCIENT AND
MODERN:

AND EMBRACING AN

## Account of the Coal and Iron Trade.

*John Nock Bagnall*

WOLVERHAMPTON:
WILLIAM PARKE, 18, HIGH STREET.
LONDON: J. MASTERS, ALDERSGATE STREET.

# Contents.

—

Arms.

ARMS. *Plate* 1

HERONVILLE.

LEVENTHORP.

COMBERFORD.

BEAUMONT.

COMBERFORD.

ARMS. *Plate 2*

HOO.

SCOTT.

PAGET.

LADY EMILY FOLEY.

ROGER WEDNESBURY.

PARKES.

HOPKINS.

ST. PAUL.

ROSE.

HOLDEN.

# List of Subscribers.

---

The Marquis of ANGLESEY, K.G., Beaudesert
Mr. George Adams, Wednesbury
John F. Adams, Esq., Darlaston
Mr. Thomas Alsop, Wednesbury
T. R. Andrews, Esq., Woodhouse
Mr. Frederick Andrews, Wolverhampton
Mr. Richard Ashmore, Wednesbury

The Earl of BRADFORD, Weston Park
Mrs. Bagnall, Monmouth
Thomas Bagnall, Esq., Great Barr (6 copies)
William Bagnall, Esq., Hamstead Hall, Handsworth (4 copies)
John N. Bagnall, Esq., West Bromwich (4 copies)
James Bagnall, Esq., West Bromwich (4 copies)
Charles Bagnall, Esq., West Bromwich (4 copies)
Thomas Bagnall, Esq., jun., West Bromwich (4 copies)
C. H. Bailey, Esq., West Bromwich (2 copies)
Mr. James Bailey, Wednesbury
Mr. Joseph Bailey, Capponfield
Edward Banks, Esq., Wolverhampton
George J. Barker, Esq., Cleveland House
Thomas Barker, Esq., Cleveland House
Horatio Barnett, Esq., Walsall
Mr. John Barnett, Capponfield

Mr. Samuel Bayley, Wednesbury, (2 copies)
Mr. Samuel Bayley, Bentley (2 copies)
William Bennitt, Esq., Stourton Hall (2 copies)
Mr. Joseph Bentley, Wednesbury
Norris Best, Esq., Bilston
Mr. William Best (2 copies)
Mr. Joseph Bevan, Capponfield
Mrs. C. Bissell, Wednesbury
Mr. E. Blakemore, Wednesbury
Mr. James Blakemore, Wednesbury
Mr. Robert Blayney, Wednesbury
Rev. Edward Bradley, Leigh
Rev. C. F. Broadbent, Vicar of Worfield
Mr. Ralph Brown, Wednesbury

Mrs. Charles Caffin, Milton Vicarage, Kent
Capponfield Church Institution
Mr. E. P. Cartwright, Upper Gornal, Sedgley
Rev. Isaac Clarkson, Vicar of Wednesbury (2 copies)
Messrs. T. and R. Cliff, Wednesbury
Rev. W. G. Cole, Wednesbury
Mr. George F. Cole, Wednesbury
Rev. John Compson, S. Mark's, Great Wyrley
Richard Cope, Esq., Ardwick, Manchester
Charles Corser, Esq., Wolverhampton
John Crowther, Esq., Wednesbury

The Earl of DARTMOUTH, Patshull
Mr. Samuel Danks, Wednesbury
Mr. Joseph Dawes, sen., Wednesbury
Mr. F. Dicken, Wednesbury
Mr. Richard Disturnell, Wednesbury
Mr. J. T. Duce, Wednesbury
Mr. W. H. Duignan, Walsall

Mr. George Albert H. Eades, Highfields, Bilston
Edward Elwell, Esq , jun., Wood Green (2 copies)

Lady EMILY FOLEY, Stoke Edith Park
Joseph Farmer, Esq., Wolverhampton
Mr. W. W. Fereday, Wolverhampton
T. W. Fletcher, Esq., M.A., F.R.S., F.S.A., &c., Lawneswood House, Stourbridge
Rev. W. B. Flowers, Oakswell Hall, Wednesbury
S. L. Forster, Esq., Wednesbury (3 copies)
Mr. John S. Frewer, Wednesbury
Mr. James Frost, Wednesbury (2 copies)
William Fleeming Fryer, Esq., the Wergs

T. W. Giffard, Esq., Chillington Hall
Rev. G. F. Gilbanks, Capponfield
Mr. William Gill, jun., Wednesbury
Rev. D. T. Gladstone, S Thomas's, Leeds
Mr. W. D. Griffin, Wolverhampton
Thomas Griffin, Esq., Tettenhall
Mr. John Griffiths, Wednesbury
Mr. S. Griffiths, Wolverhampton
Mr. Charles Grove, Wednesbury

Lord HATHERTON, Teddesley Park
Rev. A. B. Haden, Vicar of Brewood, (2 copies)
Messrs. J. and H. Haines, Willingsworth (2 copies)
John Hartley, Esq., The Oaks, Wolverhampton
Mr. Thomas Hawley, jun., Bilston
John Hay, Esq., Brewood
Mr. Henry Haycock, Capponfield
Mr. Richard Hayes, Capponfield
Isaiah Hateley, Esq., Manchester
Benjamin Hicklin, Esq., Wightwick
Henry Hill, Esq., Tettenhall
Alexander Hordern, Esq., Oxley Manor
Mr. William Horton, Wednesbury
Mr. Daniel Howard, Hill Top
Rev. F. P. B. N. Hutton, Gold's Hill, West Bromwich

Viscount INGESTRE, Ingestre Hall

Mr. Thomas Jesson, West Bromwich
Mr. John Jones, Wednesbury
William Jones, Esq., Bilston

Mr. Thomas Keay, Wednesbury

Viscount LEWISHAM, Patshull
The Lord Bishop of LICHFIELD, Eccleshall Castle
Hon. E. R. LITTLETON, M.P., Teddesley
William Lees, Esq., Trysull
Mr. Edwin Lewis, Bilston
Samuel Lloyd, Esq., Wednesbury
Samuel Lloyd, Esq., jun., Wednesbury
Sampson Lloyd, Esq., Wednesbury
Mr. W. Lloyd, Wednesbury
James Loxdale, Esq., Albrighton
Mr. C. A. Loxton, Wednesbury

Sir OSWALD MOSLEY, Bart., Rolleston Park
George Monckton, Esq., Somerford Hall
Mr. Richard Marsh, Bilston
John Marshall, Esq., Wednesbury
Rev. H. B. Mason, Bishop's Itchington
Mr. William Miles, Wednesbury
Mr. G. Millington, Capponfield
Mr. John Mitchell, Wolverhampton
R. Fryer Morson, Esq., Bloxwich
Mr. N. Moxfield, Capponfield
Mr. George H. Muntz, Wednesbury (2 copies

Mr. Joseph Nayler, Wednesbury
Mr. W. S. Nayler, Wednesbury
James Negus, Esq., Wednesbury

Mr. J. A. Palin, Wednesbury
Mrs. Parke, the Deanery, Wolverhampton

Mr. Thomas Parkes, Wednesbury
Madame Perdonnet, Mons Repos, Lausanne
F. Charles Perry, Esq., Summerfield
Mr. James S. Piercy, Wednesbury
Mr. Samuel Poole, Wednesbury

George Robinson, Esq., Wolverhampton
Mme. la Baronne de Roeder, Angermunde, Prussia
William Henry Rogers, Esq., Goldthorn
Henry Rogers, Esq., Wolverhampton
Mr. Carmi Rollason, Sedgley
Benjamin Round, Esq., Wednesbury
Mr. D. G. Round, Daisy Bank, Bilston
Charles Russell, Esq., Wednesbury
Thomas Russell, Esq., Wednesbury
John James Russell, Esq., Wednesbury

Sir FRANCIS E. SCOTT, Bart., Great Barr Hall
Sir HORACE ST. PAUL, Bart., Ewart Park (3 copies)
William Salt, Esq., Russell Square, London
Thomas Salt, Esq., Stafford
Mr. Samuel Salt, Wednesbury
Mr. Henry Scott, Wolverhampton
Mr. Frederick W. Seaman, Wednesbury
Mr. R. C. Siddons, Westbromwich
George Skey, Esq., Summerfield, Wolverhampton
Rev. J. H. Sharwood, Vicar of Walsall
John Shaw, Esq., Oxley House
Mr. J. Shorthouse, Wednesbury
Mr. Edward Smith, Wednesbury
Mr. G. H. Smith, Wednesbury
Rev. J. Finch Smith, Rector of Aldridge
James H. Smith, Esq., Brewood
Mrs. Smith, Bowden Deans, Altrincham
Mr. Joseph Smith, Wednesbury
Mr. John Smith, Wednesbury
Mr. James Solly, Wednesbury

W. Hanbury Sparrow, Esq., Penn
W. M. Sparrow, Esq., Penn Court
Arthur Sparrow, Esq., the Cedars, Penn
John W. Sparrow, Esq., Penn
Mr. John Stevens, Wednesbury

Earl Talbot, Ingestre Hall
Mr. J. F. Tart, Wednesbury
Mr. S. M. Tasker, Wednesbury
Rev. H. Taylor, Wednesbury
Thomas Thorneycroft, Esq., Tettenhall Wood
Thomas Thornely, Esq., M.P.
J. H. Thursfield, Esq., Wednesbury
Mr. J. R. Tilley, Oakham, Dudley
Mr. John Turley, Wednesbury
Rev. Richard Twigg, Wednesbury

Joseph Underhill, Esq., Newbridge

Rev. W. F. Vance, Incumbent of Coseley

John Walker, Esq., Gospel Oak Works
Edmund Walker, Esq., Gospel Oak Works
Mr. J. D. Walker, Wednesbury
Thomas Walker, Esq., Wednesbury (2 copies)
Henry Ward, Esq., Oaklands, Wolverhampton
George Ward, Esq., Oaklands, Wolverhampton
Miss Ward, Oaklands, Wolverhampton
T. Higgs Ward, Esq., Wolverhampton
W. Warner, Esq., Wolverhampton
Mr. John Watts, Wednesbury
J. W. Weaver, Esq., Oaken
Wednesbury Mechanics' Institution
Mr. A. W. Whitehouse, Wednesbury
Mr. Benjamin Whitehouse, West Bromwich
Mr. Jesse Whitehouse, Wednesbury
Mr. R. Williams, Wednesbury

**Walter Williams, Esq., West Bromwich**
J. H. Williamson, Esq., Goldenhill
Rev. J. Winter, Wednesbury
William Wood, Esq., Wednesbury
Mr. John Wood, Wednesbury
Mr. James Wood, Wednesbury
Mr. Benjamin Woodward, Wednesbury
Francis Woodward, Esq., Wednesbury.

# HISTORY OF WEDNESBURY.

## CHAPTER I.

## 𝕿𝖍𝖊 𝕬𝖓𝖈𝖎𝖊𝖓𝖙 𝕿𝖔𝖜𝖓.

𝕿𝖍𝖊 town of Wednesbury is situated near the head of the river Tame, in the southern division of the hundred of Offlow, and in the county of Stafford, and diocese of Lichfield;—distant from Stafford nineteen miles, from Lichfield twelve miles, and from Birmingham eight miles;—being bounded on the north by Walsall, the west by Bilston, the south-west by Sedgley and Tipton, the north-west by Darlaston, and on the south by West Bromwich.

In the time of the Ancient Britons, it was, doubtless, a station of some importance. Its natural position, as well as its vicinity to the residence of the Druid-priests at Barr, and many other similar adjacent sites, would recommend it, in an especial manner, as a place of resort. A hill, such as the one on which the town of Wednesbury stands, —midway between the beacons of Barr and Sedgley, occupying, as it does, a most commanding situation in the

B

midst of an open country, and abounding in the sacred oak,—would cause it to be highly venerated by the Druids and their followers, by reason of an idea which then obtained, that the tops of hills made a nearer approach to the heavens, from whence the Deity could more perfectly hear their prayers, and the more readily comply with their wants; hence the most mountainous tracts in Britain were universally selected by the aborigines for places of habitation, and thereby became thickly peopled in comparison with other parts, so that in process of time every solitary hill formed the abode of a colony of native Britons.

The early history of Britain is probably involved in greater obscurity than that of any other nation. Divers causes may be assigned for this fact—any *one* of which would in itself be sufficient to account for the paucity of materials that exists. The exclusive character of the Druidical religion—the jealousy that existed of foreign interference— the custom of using *mystic* characters and signs—as also the incessant disquietude that marked the period now referred to,—a disquietude arising from internal feuds and external invasions,—all combined to bury in oblivion the traditions connected with the country, and to destroy whatever histories might at one time be extant relating to it. If then the difficulties and disadvantages are so great in obtaining information concerning a country as a *whole*, they must be even greater with respect to a *component* part of that country.

This must be considered as a sufficient excuse for not giving any information, except in general terms, of the period to which we are now referring, or even until some centuries after the commencement of the Christian era; but should the reader wish to become acquainted with an ac- count of the Druids,—and of the religion of the ancient

inhabitants of Wednesbury,—he is directed to consult
" Cæsar's Commentaries," " Tacitus' Annals," and the writ-
ings of Ptolemy of Alexandria—of Diodorus Siculus ; as
also the Pharsalia of Lucan. We would briefly mention
here, however, that these authors relate " that this island
was the stronghold of Druidism—a system of religion which
bound together, in a marvellous manner, the various king-
doms, tribes, and families, which were swayed by its tenets ;
that the chief object of worship was the oak tree, from
whence they derive their name—' δρυς' in Greek, and ' Drui'
in Celtic, signifying tree ;* that fire and water, the sun,
moon, and stars, received Divine honours ; and that the
serpent was an especial object of veneration, insomuch that
the serpent's egg or *anguinum* is mentioned by Pliny as
having been worn by the arch-Druid as *the* badge of office."†
They likewise inform us, that the Druids believed in the
transmigration of the soul, and that this doctrine was carefully instilled into the young in order to make them regard-
less of death, and, therefore courageous in the time of
battle. Diogenes Laertius acquaints us that the substance
of their system of faith and practice was comprised in three
precepts, viz.: to *worship the gods, to do no evil, and to behave
courageously*. But the simplest, truest, and most ancient
form of worship of the Druids appears to have been the
worship of the celestial luminaries and of fire. " *Under every
green tree, and on every high hill*" were the altars of the sun
and moon reared, and, as the fire consumed the victim, the

* Here, then, we find that the "Dryades" of the Ancient Greeks is but another
name for the " Druidhe" of the Ancient Britons—the former having the appellation of
the *sylvan* nymphs, the latter of the *sylvan* priests.

† The prevalence of this superstition throughout many nations evinces its deriva-
tion from the most ancient tradition of the human race—a tradition which took its
rise at the fall of man.—See History of England.

deluded priest and people shouted for joy that another mortal had been received into the ranks and number of the stars.

As the Druids were *the priests*, so likewise were they *the judges*. No cause, ecclesiastical or civil, was tried in any other court than theirs; and the judgment of the arch-Druid, after consulting with his subordinates, was deemed definitive; there was no appeal—his word was law. Thus the supreme power was in the hands of the priesthood: " they slew whom they would; and whom they would they saved alive." The influence they possessed over the minds of the entire nation was immense: their sway was universal —their rule despotic.

Matters were in this state in the year B.C. 55, when Julius Cæsar crossed over from Gaul and landed upon the shores of Britain, *ostensibly* for the purpose of collecting pearls, *virtually* in order to subdue this nursery and hot-bed of Druidism, which constantly fomented the spirit of rebellion in the conquered province of Gaul. After the subjugation of the kingdom, Wednesbury, with its natural advantages, in all probability, would not be overlooked by the Romans; and from the fact of the great military road of Ikneild Street running within a few miles, and from the further fact of coin, bearing the impress of Nero, Vespasian, and Trajan, having been discovered in the parish, this probability amounts to a moral certainty.

The Romans, after a hard struggle with the persevering natives, were finally compelled to evacuate the Island,* leaving a party behind them in favour of their rule. Between this party and the patriotic British a civil war arose, in which the latter, under the leadership of Vortigern, were worsted; but recovering somewhat, however, from the

* A.D. 440.

effects of their defeat, they determined to call to their
assistance the Saxons, a warlike people who lived in the
north of Germany, and the Jutes and Angles, who inhabited Denmark. The Saxons having thus obtained a footing
in the country proceeded to subjugate it to their sway—a
process which required 150 years to accomplish, whereupon
England was divided into seven portions, viz.: Kent, Northumberland, East Anglia, Mercia, Essex, Sussex, and
Wessex. Mercia, in which Wednesbury was situated, com-
prehended all the midland counties, and formed the *largest*
if not the most *powerful* division of the Heptarchy.

The Saxons, equally alive with the Romans to the commanding position of certain situations, were not likely to
overlook the martial advantages of Wednesbury. This is
fully proved by the origin of the name itself,—Wednesbury being derived from the compound Wodens-beorg,*—
"Woden" being the Saxon God of War, and "beorg"
signifying a hill or mountain, or otherwise from "burg,"
which signifies a fortified place. This is further confirmed
by the researches of an eminent antiquarian† who states
"that the Saxons were extremely partial to the Roman
foundations in Britain, to which, when they occupied them,
they gave the appellation of "burgh," implying in its primitive signification a "place of strength." The Saxon "burgs"
or towns were of *royal creation* . . . and defended with
walls or castles;" and we find from Doomsday Book that
Wednesbury, previous to the Norman Conquest, belonged to
the *Saxon monarchs*.

On referring to the few remaining Anglo-Saxon chronicles,
and through the kindness of a celebrated Saxon linguist,‡
(the originals having been carefully searched) we are

* Vide Marsh, vol. ii., p. 465.     † Hinderwell: History of Scarboro'.
‡ The Rev. Dr. Giles.

enabled to trace the earlier history of Wednesbury to about 400 years before the Norman Conquest, or about 1180 years from the present time. Therein we read, that in the year 591 or 592, a battle having been fought at " Wodnesbeorg," between Ceawlin, the ambitious King of Wessex, and the Britons, there was a great slaughter, which resulted in the defeat of the former, who died shortly after, and was succeeded by his nephew Ceolric. Also in the year 715, Ina, King of Wessex, fought with Ceolrid, King of Mercia, at " Wothnesbeorg," when the battle was undecided. Towards the end of the Heptarchy (which prevailed from about the year 585 to 800) the Danes, who were then a nation of pirates, invaded the kingdom for the purpose of plunder, and committed dreadful ravages. They repeated their invasions from time to time, until they became masters of the kingdom, when three of their princes were numbered among the sovereigns of England.

When Edward the Elder ascended the throne, the country was almost equally divided between the English and the Danes. Ethelred, Earl of Mercia, and the Princess Ethelfleda, his wife (the daughter of our Great Alfred,) were of eminent service to the king in prosecuting the war in which he was engaged, (A.D. 903), by making head against the Mercian Danes, and preventing the Welsh from coming to their aid. Ethelward, who laid claim to the crown after the death of Alfred, applied to France for assistance, and received powerful aid from the Normans, who, on landing, roused the Danes of Northumberland and East Anglia, and caused them to espouse his cause. These Danes took up arms against the king, threw themselves into Mercia, and ravaged the country inhabited by the English in a merciless manner. The king put himself at the head of his army and gave them battle, and after repeated victories Ethelward was slain; but the war was carried on two years after his death. The Danes, at last, were obliged to sue for peace, which the king readily granted on conditions; but, at the end of three years the war was renewed. However it proved fatal to the Danes. In a very short time they lost two battles,—one fought at Wednesfield, in which were several thousand Danes slain, with the Kings Ecwils and Halfden,—the other at Tettenhall, near Wolverhampton. The king followed up his success by completely driving them out of the kingdom of Mercia. It was then that Ethelred, who had so much assisted the king, his brother-in-law, became in reality Earl of Mercia; he died however soon after.

Ethelfleda now took upon herself the government of Mercia. Following the example of her father, and of the king, her brother, in fortifying towns, she was determined that the Danes should not settle in Mercia again. She therefore fortified Wednesbury about the year 916,* and built a castle on the hill at present occupied by the parish church. Besides this, she likewise constructed the castles of Bridgnorth, Tamworth, Stafford, and Warwick, with several others within the kingdom of Mercia. When she had taken these precautions, she carried her arms into Wales, and, after several victories, obliged the Welsh to become her tributaries. Ingulph says—"That in respect of the cities Ethelfleda built, the castles she fortified, and the armies she managed, it might have been thought she had changed her sex." Ethelfleda—and we may mention also Leofwin—had great possessions in Mercia. The latter was the powerful Earl of Chester and of Mercia, and husband of the celebrated Godiva, who liberated Coventry. Soon after the erection of the castle at Wednesbury, Ethelfleda died

* Florence of Worcester.

at Tamworth, and was buried in the east porch of S. Peter's
Church—now the cathedral—in Gloucester.

The Anglo-Saxon chronicles guide us no further; and we
have no certain information of the ancient town until after
the country had passed through its transition stage from the
Saxon rule to that of the Norman. William the Norman
having subjugated the kingdom, became possessed, by right
of conquest, of all the property belonging to the ancient
Saxon kings, in which Wednesbury, being a royal demesne,
was included. This leads us to give some account of the
feudal system and the History of

## The Manor.

Soon after the conquest of the country by the Saxons, it
was found necessary by the large landed proprietors to
retain a great body of warriors, in order to defend their
demesnes from the inroads, as well of hostile chieftains,
as of the native British. The land was accordingly divided
into two portions; the one part was given to the kindred
and free retainers of the proprietors, who gave in return
military service; the remaining part was parcelled out into
different farms, and committed to the management of particular bondmen, from whom a strict account of the produce
was required at the end of the year. Ultimately the former
class came to be styled "vassals" the latter "villains."

The feudal estates* or manors appear *originally* to have
been held during the will of the superior—*then* for a deter-
minate time—*afterwards* for life—and *finally* to have been
hereditary; the only proviso being,—that the person granting

* Sir Francis Palgrave.

the land should be faithfully served and supported by him to whom the land was granted.

The Anglo-Saxons, in common with other Teutonic nations, were divided into various castes or ranks. The highest of these was that from whènce the king was chosen; the second were the nobility who were earls or *thane born;* the third rank was composed of the remainder of the people, and consisted of the *ceorls* or *villains.*

The *theowes*—the *servi* of Doomsday—were entirely destitute of political right; they did not rank among the people. Some of them were no doubt the offspring of the British serfs, but the majority consisted of free men who had forfeited their liberty by their crimes.

The *bordarii,* or borderers, appear in a great measure to correspond with these latter; the only difference that can be discovered between them being, that the *theowes* were slaves from the commission of crime, the borderers slaves by right of conquest or purchase. The different classes were all subject unto the king, who was elected from the first order, and claimed descent from the deified monarch of the Asi, Odin or Woden.

The Conquest of Britain by the Normans produced no improvement in the feudal system, but on the contrary strengthened it greatly, as thereby the conquerors were the better enabled to keep the Saxons in subjection. But what gave the crown the most influence, and produced the largest revenue, were the profits arising from the manors, fourteen of which belonged exclusively to the king. The servants of the crown, placed in these strongholds—up and down the country, and throughout the length and breadth of the land —proved a formidable police, and served as well to keep the impetuous spirit of the various chieftains in check, as, also, to observe and report whatever might be going on in the provinces. These manors, with that of Wednesbury, were, with the crown, ceded to the Conqueror, who exercised the same authority over them as the ancient kings had done before.*

An interesting survey of the whole of England, with the exception of the four northern counties, viz.:—Westmoreland, Northumberland, Durham, Cumberland, and part of Lancashire, was made by the order of King William the Norman. It was commenced in the year 1080, and completed in 1086, the commissioners appointed for the purpose having fully and faithfully accomplished their task. The result is found in "Doomsday Book," from which the following extract has been taken, viz.:—" The king retains Wadnesberrie, with the appurtenances. It contains three hides.† The arable land is nine carucates ‡—one in demesne, and one servant, and sixteen villains, and eleven borderers, have seven carucates. There is a mill of 2s. rent, and one acre of meadow; also a wood, two miles in length and one in breadth."|| According to the same authority there were, in the county of Stafford, 330 towns, villages, or hamlets; whereof the king retained 55 of the best, granting to the clergy 97, and to the laity 178.

The manor of Wednesbury remained in the possession of the crown until about the reign of Henry II., when it was transferred to the ancestors of William Heronville, in exchange for the town of Stuntsfield, in Oxfordshire. This interesting fact agrees with what is more fully recorded in the curious tenure roll of the hundred of Offlow, in the time of Henry III., (A.D. 1255,) which states that " Simon de Heronville holds the manor of Wednesbury of the heir of

* Pictorial History of England.
† Hide. An uncertain quantity of land, generally about 120 acres.
‡ Carucate, carve, or ploughland. Generally 100 acres.
|| Bloxwich was a member of the same manor.

Henry d'Oylli, and was aforetime a demesne of the king, and given in exchange, to the ancestors of the said Simon, for the town of Stuntsfield, near Woodstock, and pays annually to the lord the king 20s. 20d. ; for the manor of Wonnesbury was worth so much more than Stuntsfield when the exchange was made. It has a free court and view of frankpledge, [*] but it is not known by what warrant; and pays 3s. to the sheriff for view of frankpledge, and owes suit at the 2 hundred courts to ask for its own free court. There is in the said manor one hide, and it is worth £12 per annum."

The manor next passed to William Leventhorpe, by virtue of his marriage with Joan, daughter and heiress of Henry Heronville, about A.D. 1421. Their daughter Joan carried this and other estates in marriage to Sir Henry Beaumont, Knight, brother to John Viscount Beaumont, slain at Northampton A.D. 1460, and was descended from that very ancient family, whose ancestor was son of Louis VIII. King of France.

The manor then came into the possession of the Comberford family, by the marriage of Humphrey Comberford, of Comberford, with Dorothy, second daughter of John Beaumont, who died A.D. 1502. At this time the manor and estate were valued at £13 14s. 4d.

A person of the name of Gilpin having purchased the manor from the Comberfords, sold it shortly after to John Shelton, of Birmingham.

About the year 1710, the son of John Shelton sold it to John Hoo, of Bradley, sergeant-at-law. From him the inheritance fell into the hands of his brother Joseph, who contracting marriage with Jane Vaughton, widow, had issue two sons, John and Thomas. John Hoo, dying without issue,

1749, was succeeded by his brother Thomas, of Barr, who died, childless, September, 1791 :—thence the manor descended, in the female line, to Mrs. Whitby and the Honourable Mrs. Foley, who are now represented by Sir Francis Scott, of Great Barr, Bart., and Lady Emily Foley, of Stoke Edith, widow of the late E. T. Foley, Esq., and daughter of the third Duke of Montrose, a nobleman representing one of the oldest and best of the Scottish families.

The ancient Manor House is situated near the parish church, to the north-east, and is now converted into a farm house, retaining nothing of its former magnificence. It is at the present time the property of Sir H. St. Paul, Bart.

Wednesbury is governed by a constable, chosen annually, at a manorial court, held in October, together with headboroughs, overseers of fields and hedges, and victual and ale tasters.

# Appendix to the Manor.

---

*Record Office, Tower of London.*

*Inquisitio post mortem*, 8th *Edward II.*, No. 34.

INQUISICIO de terris et tenementis de quibus Johannes de Heronvill fuit seisitus in dominico suo ut de feodo die quo obiit, videlicet quantum terre idem Johannes tenuit de herede Hugonis de Plessetis defuncti, qui de Domino Edwardo quondam Rege Anglie patre Domini Regis qui nunc est, tenuit in capite infra etatem et in custodia Domini Regis existente tenuit per servicium militare et quantum de aliis et per quod servicium, et quantum terre et tenementa illa valeant per annum in omnibus exitibus et quis propinquior heres ejus sit et cujus etatis, Facta coram Escaetore apud Wodnesbury vij die Februarii anno regni Regis Edwardi octavo, per sacramentum Willielmi de Wanore, Willielmi atte Wode, Willielmi de Honesworthe, Willielmi de Derlastone, Thome Hyllary, Ricardi le Rugaker, Ade atte Ree, Nicholai Golde, Ricardi le Grete, Ade Torel, Willielmi Moysaunt et Nicholai de Luttelham Juratorum, Qui dicunt super sacramentum suum quod predictus Johannes nihil tenuit die quo obiit de predicto herede Hugonis de Plessetis qui in custodia Domini Regis existit sed tenuit die quo obiit manerium de Wodnesbury de Domino Rege in capite in exscambio pro manerio de Stuntesfeld in Comitatu Oxonie, et quia'manerium de Wodnesbury plus valuit quam manerium de Stuntesfeld, servatur manerium de Wodnesbury de xx. solidis ad Saccarium Domini Regis solvendis per manus vice comitis Staffordie per annum. Et sic tenuit manerium predictum sine aliquo servicio inde faciendo preterquam illos xx solidos per annum. In quo manerio capitale messuagium cum gardinis et curtilagiis valet per annum ij^s. et sunt ibidem due carucate terre arrabilis que continent vi^xx acras terre que valent per annum xx solidos precium acre ij denarij, et habuit in eodem Manerio unum Messuagium quod Thomas Trond aliquando tenuit et valet per annum vi denarios, ad quod messuagium pertinet dimidium virgate terre quod continet xv. acras terre que valent ij* vij denarios precium acre ij denarij, et ad hoc pertinet duas acras* prati que valent per annum xij denarios precium acre vj denarij. Et sunt in manerio predicto x acre prati que valent per annum v solidos, precium (acre) vi denarij. Et est ibidem quoddam molendinum aquaticum quod valet per annum cum vivario vi solidos viij denarios. Et est ibidem unum columbare quod valet per annum ij solidos. Et est ibidem una placea pasture separalis que valet per annum ij solidos. Et est ibidem de Redditu Assiso liberorum tenentium L solidi ij denarij. Et est ibidem de reddituo assiso xxiij custumariorum LX solidi i denarius obolus. Et est ibidem de redditu cotrellorum xxi solidi. Et isti redditus solvi debent ad quatuor anni terminos videlicet ad Festa annunciacionis beate Marie, Nativitatis beati Johannis Sancti Michaelis et Sancti Andrie Apostoli equis porcionibus. Item dicunt quod placita et perquisita curie ibidem valent per annum i solidum. Et dicunt quod Henricus de Heronvile filius predicti Johannis est propinquior heres ejusdem Johannis et fuit etatis quinquaginta annorum in Festo Sancti Michaelis ultimo preterito. In cujus rei testimonium predicti Jurati huic Inquisicioni sigilla sua apposuerunt.

Predictus Johês nullas alias terras nec tenementa tenuit in balliva mea die quo obiit nisi terras et tenementa in ista inquisicione contenta.

———

*Record Office, Tower of London.*

### Stafford.

Assignacio dotis Juliane que fuit uxor Johannis de Heronville, videlicet de omnibus terris et tenementis que fuerunt prefati Johannis quondam viri sui facta coram Escaetore Domini Regis apud Wednesbury decimo die Marcij anno regni Regis Edwardi viijº· per sacramentum Thome de Derlaston, Johannis Dymmoge, Rogeri Basset, Willielmi de . . . . . Philippi Attehalle et Hugonis de Grete.

Primitus assignatur eidem quedam aula cum pantera cum veteri solario et celario juxta coquinam cum bracina et quadam domo que vocatur le Knedhous et medietas stab . . hospicij versus boveriam et quedam

* Sic.

camera ultra portas cum medietate longe bercarie sicut bundatur. Et assignatur eidem media pars gardini cum curtilagio et media pars de Lenlibzart cum libero introitu et exitu ad omnes domos et particulas predictas ad dictam aulám assignatas. Et quod illa placea terre que jacet inter aulam et coquinam in latitudine et inter solarium et le Knedhous in longitudine utrique parti sit communis una cum aysiamentis fontis. Et quod curia extrainseca pro in diviso habeatur sed utrique parti sit communis. Et assignatur eidem tercia pars cujusdam columbarij. Et assignatur eidem quedam pars cujusdam grangie apud Tronteslond versus bercariam sicut bundatur cum tercia parte cujusdam placee terre ibidem sicut bundatur. Et assignantur eidem xvj seliones terre in Momweyesfeld in medio sicut bundatur. Et assignantur eidem . . seliones terre et dimidium in Cheresmorefforlong in medio. Et in eodem campo superius viij seliones terre in medio, et in la Dale ij seliones terre sicut bundantur . . . . dio. Et assignatur eidem v seliones terre in Ladicroft versus boveriam, et x seliones terre in Ladicroft juxta Alradeswalle in medio, et x seliones terre in Ladicroft juxta Kyngeshullestone in medio sicut bundantur. Et vij butti ibidem in medio sicut bundantur. Et assignantur eidem ij seliones terre in medio de Depesiche et ij butti ibidem in medio sicut bundantur et ij seliones terre de le Welbelond apud Rugewestile et ij seliones in eadem . . . . Et ij seliones super Blakemunlde in parte boreali, et una selio in . . . parte australi juxta Bradeswalle versus le Colpetes sicut bundantur. Et assignantur eidem ij seliones terre in Aycaker juxta Wedneswalle, et vij seliones terre in . . . . in medio, et in le medwezart viij seliones terre in medio sicut bundantur et in le Morforlong una selio in medio versus occidentem. Et assignantur (eidem) iiij seliones terre in nova placea terre in medio juxta Godithescrofte et ix seliones terre in Godithescrofte in parte orientali et vii butti sicut . . . . Et assignantur eidem vi seliones terre in le Hordewyke in parte australi et una placea terre in Wetecrofte versus Monithorn sicut bundatur, et . . . terre in Kyngeshullefforlong in parte boreali, et assignantur eidem v seliones terre in Monithornefforlong in parte boreali, et iij seliones terre in . . . . in parte orientali, et v seliones terre in le Hallefeld in medio sub gardino, et ii seliones terre et ii butti in parte orientali subtus aulam et v . . . in cultura que vocatur le Preestesthorn in medio sicut bundantur et iij seliones terre subtus domum Thome Attedelf in medio cum et vi seliones terre in le Stockynge in medio, et viij seliones terre in le Rudyngge in medio sicut bundantur, et xi seliones terre . . . . in medio et viij seliones in eodem campo sicut bundantur, et xi seliones terre et xii butti in Bruche apud Bernestite in parte orientali (sicut) bundantur, et assignantur eidem ii seliones terre in le Moniweyeffeld apud Leybrocke, et iij seliones terre abovethedale in . . . selio ibidem in parte australi. Et assignantur eidem iij seliones terre et unum buttum in Apeltrefforlonge in parte orientali. Et ij seliones . . . . crabbetree, et iij seliones terre versus croftum Alexandri sicut bundantur: Et una selio in Chirchefeld versus domum Thome Bonde in parte australi, et . . . . juxta le Perie in parte orientali sicut bundatur. Et assignatur eidem media pars de Welbelaxstone sicut bundatur et media pars campi quod fuit Johannis Brevile sicut bundatur. Et assignatur eidem tercia pars piscarie omnium marleriarum.

Et assignatur eidem quedam pars de Sprynggeswalle medwe versus Monewey sicut bundatur. Et media pars de Alradeswallewey *weltromene* medwe, most mormedwe, Godichrofmedwe et tercia pars de Aldecroft le Erdyngge sicut bundantur, et assignatur eidem media pars cuiusdam vasti super Pekehet et media pars de Gerneyse Heye sicut bundantur.

Et assignatur eidem tercia pars cuiusdam molendini aquatici qui* valet per annum vi$^a$· viiij$^d$·

Et assignatur eidem tercia pars cuiusdam minerie ferri que valet per annum vi$^a$·

Et assignantur eidem xix$^s$· ix$^d$· de redditu assiso liberorum tenentium videlicet de Willielmo Golde v$^d$· De Johanne filio Reginaldi xii$^d$· De Hugone Grete viii$^a$· De Johanne Attehalle iiij$^a$ ij$^d$· De Ricardo de Grete ij$^d$· De Johanne Dymmoge ij$^a$·viiij$^d$·, De Thoma Bonde xiiij$^d$·, De Willielmo de Luttelhaye vi$^d$·, De Ricardo le ffremon vi$^d$·, De Johanne le Somiter nil, De Rogero Illary xiiij$^d$·, De Johanne de Herunville iiij$^d$·

Et assignantur eidem xxiij$^s$·xj$^d$· ob. quad. de redditu Custumariorum videlicet De Thoma de Erbury ij$^a$·viij$^d$·, De Ricardo Attegrene ij$^a$·vi$^d$·, De Henrico Atteldrate iiij$^a$· vi$^d$·, De Henrico le Palmare ij$^a$· iiij$^d$· De Ricardo le Rowe xiij$^d$·, De Ricardo Atteoke iiij$^a$· vi$^d$· ob. quad. De Willielmo filio Walteri iiij$^a$· iij$^d$·, De Thoma Attedelf iiij$^a$·

Et assignantur eidem v$^a$· x$^d$· quad. de redditu cotrellorum. videlicet De Ricardo Podynge vi$^d$· ob. de Thoma filio Henrici xiij$^d$· De Willielmo le Camherde, . . . . De Willielmo filio Radulphi vi$^d$· De Philippo Nightyngale iiij$^d$· De Johanne Cloke ix$^d$· De Waltero de Luttlehay iiij$^d$·

* Sic.

*Record Office, Tower of London.*

### Inquisitio post mortem 9th Edward II.

Edwardus, Dei gracia, Rex Anglie Dominus Hibernie et Dux Aquitanie dilecto clerico suo Magistro Johanni Walewayn Escaetori suo citra Trentam, salutem. Quia Henricus de Heronville qui de nobis tenuit in capite, diem clausit extremum, ut accepimus, vobis mandamus quod omnes terras et tenementa de quibus idem Henricus fuit seisitus in dominico suo ut de feodo in balliva vestra die quo obiit sine dilacione capiatis in manum nostram et ea salva custodiri faciatis donec aliud inde precepimus. Et per sacramentum proborum et legalium hominum de balliva vestra, per quos rei veritatem melius sciri poterit diligenter inquiratis quantum terre idem Henricus tenuit de nobis in capite in balliva vestra die quo obiit et quantum de aliis et per quod servicium, et quantum terre ille valeant per annum in omnibus exitibus et quis propinquior heres ejus sit et cujus etatis. Et inquisicionem inde distincte et aperte factam nobis sub sigillo vestro et sigillis eorum per quos facta fuerit sine dilacione mittatis et hoc breve. Teste me ipso apud Westmonasterium tercio die Maij anno regni nostri nono.

---

*Record Office, Tower of London.*

### Inquisitio post mortem, 9th Edward II.

### Stafford.

Inquisicio facta coram Escaetore Domini Regis apud Wednesbury x. die Maij anno regni Regis Edwardi nono, videlicet de omnibus terris et tenementis de quibus Henricus de Herunville fuit seisitus ut de feodo die quo obiit, per sacramentum Willielmi Golde, Johannis Dymmog, Rogeri Basset, Willielmi Golde, Willielmi de Littlehay, Thome Bonde, Henry de Mockeslowe, Rogeri Golde, Galfridi Henrici, Johannis Attewolle, Rogeri de Bringhulle et Johannis le Someter Qui dicunt super sacramentum suum quod idem Henricus tenuit de Domino Rege in capite in comitatu predicto die quo obiit Manerium de Wednesbury in exscambium pro Manerio de Stuntesfield per servicium xx solidorum ad saccarium Domini Regis de quo quidem Manerio de Wednesbury Juliana de Herunville dotata est de tercia parte dicti Manerij, et sunt ibidem due partes unius messuagii que valent per annum vj$^d$ gardina et curtilagium que valent per annum

**D**

xij<sup>d.</sup> et sunt ibidem xl acre terre que valent per annum in omnibus exitibus
xl<sup>d.</sup> precium acre unum denarium, et sunt ibidem iij acre prati que valent
per annum iij solidos, precium acre xij<sup>d.</sup> et sunt ibidem iiij acre pasture
que valent per annum ij<sup>s.</sup> precium acre vj<sup>d.</sup>, et sunt ibidem due partes unius
columbarij precium vj<sup>d.</sup> et sunt ibidem due partes unius molendini aquatici
que valent per annum ij<sup>s.</sup> et est ibidem de redditu assiso per annum de
liberis tenentibus in dicto manerio xxxix<sup>s.</sup> vj<sup>d.</sup> et est ibidem de redditu
custumariorum per annum xlvij<sup>s.</sup> x<sup>d.</sup> ob. et est ibidem de redditu coterel-
lorum per annum xj<sup>s.</sup> viij<sup>d.</sup> ob· solvenda ad terminos subscriptos videlicet
ad festa Sancti Michaelis, Sancti Andrei Apostoli, Annunciacionis beate
Marie et sancti Johannis Baptiste equis porcionibus, et sunt ibidem
placita et perquisita curie que valent per annum xij<sup>d.</sup>, Item dicunt quod
idem Henricus tenuit de Matilda Burnell unum Messuagium apud Tibyn-
ton in eodem Comitatu quod valet per annum iiij<sup>d.</sup>, et sunt ibidem xij acre
terre que valent per annum xij<sup>d.</sup>, precium acre j<sup>d.</sup>, et est ibidem una acra
prati que valet viiij<sup>d.</sup> per annum, et est ibidem quedam placea pasture que
valet per annum xl<sup>d.</sup> et est ibidem de redditu assiso per annum x<sup>s.</sup> et
reddet inde Matilda Burnell per annum iiij<sup>s.</sup> ad duos anni terminos. Item
dicunt quod Johannes filius Henrici de Herunville est propinquior heres
ejusdem Henrici et est etatis duodecim annorum. In cujus rei testimonium predicti jurati huic Inquisicioni sigilla sua apposuerunt.

Prefatus Henricus de Heronville nullas alias terras seu tenementa
tenuit in dominico suo ut de feodo in balliva mea die quo obiit nisi terras
et tenementa in ista inquisicione contenta.

---

*Record Office, Tower of London.*

*Close Roll, 9th Edward II., membrane 6.*

### *De fidelitate capta.*

Rex dilecto Clerico suo magistro Johanni Walewayn, Escaetori suo
citra Trentam, salutem. Quia accepimus per inquisicionem quam per vos
fieri fecimus quod Henricus de Heronville defunctus tenuit de nobis in
capite die quo obiit Manerium de Wednesbury cum pertinenciis in
exscambium pro manerio de Stuntesfeld per servicium viginti solidorum, et
quod non tenuit aliquas alias terras seu tenementa de nobis in capite die
obitus sui, quodque Johannes filius predicti Henrici est heres eius propinquior et etatis duodecim annorum cepimus fidelitatem ipsius Johannis de

Manerio predicto. Et ideo vobis mandamus quod eidem Johanni manerium prædictum cum pertinenciis quod occasione mortis prædicti Henrici cepistis in manum nostram liberetis. De aliis terris et tenementis que idem Henricus tenuit de aliis dominis in balliva vestra die prædicto et que occasione etc. vos ulterius non intromittatis. Salvo in omnibus jure nostro. Teste Rege apud Waltham xx die Maij.

------

*Record Office, Tower of London.*

*Inquisitio post mortem, 28th Edward III.—No. 9.*

Inquisicio capta coram Johanne de Swynnerton Escaetore Domini Regis in comitatu Staffordie, die martis proximo post festum nativitatis sancti Johannis Baptiste anno Regni Regis Edwardi tercij post conquestum xxviij. per sacramentum Reginaldi de Newport, Ricardi de Waner, Nicholai le Peyntour, Roberti de Derlastone, Henrici de Mokeslowe, Johannis Bonde, Johannis Wilkyns, Ricardi le Harper, Johannis del Grene, Johannis Delowe, Thome Golde et Johannis le Waiters, qui dicunt super sacramentum suum quod Johannes de Herouill tenuit de Domino Rege in capite et in dominico die quo obiit manerium de Wednesbury cum pertinenciis in Wednesbury per servicium reddendi annuatim Domino Regi viginti unum solidos et octo denarios ad duos anni terminos, videlicet ad festa Annunciacionis beate Marie Virginis et Sancti Michaelis per equales porciones pro omnibus serviciis, et dicunt quod nihil tenuit de Domino Rege in servicio, et dicunt quod dictum manerium de Wednesbury cum pertinenciis valet per annum in omnibus exitibus centum solidos, et dicunt quod idem Johannes tenuit die quo obiit quintam partem manerij de Tibyntone cum pertinenciis in Tibyntone de Nicholao Burnell in capite et in dominico per servicium militare, reddendo inde annuatim quatuor solidos ad supradictos, terminos per equales porciones, et dicunt quod dicta quinta pars manerij de Tibyntone predicto valet per annum xiij⁺ et iiij⁴ in omnibus exitibus, salvis reprisis, et nihil de predicto Nicholao tenuit in dominico, nec de aliis in dominico nec in servicio die quo obiit, et dicunt quod idem Johannes Herouille obiit viij⁰ Junij ultimo præterito, et quod Johannes filius Johannis Herouille predicti propinquior heres ejus est, et est etatis viginti quatuor annorum et ultra. In cujus rei testimonium predicti jurati huic inquisicioni sigilla sua apposuerunt.

*Record Office, Tower of London.*

## *Inquisitio post mortem, 4th Henry IV.—No 17.*

Inquiscio capta apud Walshale coram Willielmo de Walshale Escaetore Domini Regis in Comitatu Staffordie virtute cuiusdam brevis Domini Regis eidem Escaetori directi et huic Inquisicioni consuti die Martis proxima post ffestum sancti Gregorii Pape anno regni Regis Henrici quarti post conquestum quarto per sacramentum Johannis Wylkys de Derlastone, Thome Chylternes, Ricardi Harper de Derlastone, Laurensii Happeford, Johannis Hogets, Willielmi Harper, Johannis Symcokes, Willielmi Colyns, Willielmi Swetecoke, Rogeri de Nortone, Johannis Pert de Bromwych et Thome Gylkys de Brerely. Qui dicunt super sacramentum suum quod Johannes Heruyle in brevi nominatus tenuit de Domino Rege die quo obiit manerium de Wednesbury cum pertinenciis in predicto comitatu Staffordie de dono et ffeoffamento quorundam Henrici de Tymmore parsone ecclesie de Elleford et Johannis de Tymmore factis eidem Johanni Heruyle et cujdam Alicie uxoris eiusdem Johannis Heruyle et heredibus de corporibus eorundem Johannis Heruyle et Alicie exeuntibus licencia Domini Edwardi nuper Regis Anglie avi Domini Regis nunc inde obtenta per servicium xx$^a$ eidem Domino Regi ad saccarium suum ad Festum Sancti Michaelis annuatim per manus vice comitis comitatus predicti qui pro tempore fuerit pro omnibus serviciis solvendorum; quod quidem manerium valet per annum in omnibus exitibus juxta verum valorem ejusdem ultra reprisas x$^{rm}$ Et dicunt quod predicti Johannes Heruyle et Alicia habuerunt exitum inter se quendam Henricum, et quod predicta Alicia postea obiit, et quod predictus Johannes Heruyle obiit scilicet die Veneris proxima post Festum Sancti Valentini anno regni regis supradicto, et ulterius dicunt quod predictus Henricus est filius et hæres ejusdem Johannis Heruyle propinquior et etatis triginta annorum et amplius, et quod predictus Johannes Heruyle nullas alias terras seu tenementa in dicto comitatu Staffordie tenuit de Domino Rege seu de aliis in dominico nec in servicio predicto die quo obiit. In cujus rei testimonium predicti juratores huic inquiscioni sigilla sua apposuerunt. Data die et anno supradictis.

---

*Record Office, Tower of London.*

## *Inquisicio post mortem, 7th Henry IV.—No. 81.*

Inquisicio capta apud Wolvernehamptone xxix die Septembris anno regni Regis Henrici quarti post conquestum septimo, coram Johanne

Delves Escaetore Domini Regis in comitatu Staffordie virtute brevis Domini Regis eidem Escaetori directi et huic inquisicioni consuti per sacramentum Willielmi Sponne, Johannis Welles, Johannis de Tymmore, Johannis Sneth, Ricardi Higson, Willielmi Aylwyn, Reginaldi Hemylle, Johannis Paynell, Johannis Aylemond, Ricardi atte Oke, Thome Gosebroke et Willielmi Coler Juratorum. Qui dicunt super sacramentum suum quod Henricus Herville in dicto brevi nominatus tenuit die quo obiit Manerium de Wednesbury cum pertinenciis in comitatu Staffordie in dominico suo ut de feodo de Domino Rege per servicium reddendi eidem Domino Regi viginti solidos annuatim ad saccarium in Festo Sancti Michaelis per manus vice comitis comitatus predicti . . . tempore fuerit pro omnibus serviciis quod quidem manerium cum pertinenciis suis valet per annum in omnibus exitibus juxta verum valorem ejusdem ultra reprisas x^rm. Item dicunt quod predictus Henricus Herville tenuit in dominico suo ut de feodo die quo obiit xl acras terre, xx acras bosci et x solidatûs redditus cum pertinenciis in Tibyntone in dicto comitatu de Hugone Burnell milite in socagio que quidem terre boscus et redditus cum suis pertinenciis nihil valent per annum ultra reprisas. Et dicunt quod predictus Henricus obiit die Sabbati proximo ante Festum Sancti Mathei Apostoli ultimo preterito, et quod Johanna, Alicia et Margareta filie predicti Henrici sunt heredes ejusdem propinquiores, et quod predicta Johanna est etatis quatuor annorum et amplius, et dicta Alicia est etatis duorum annorum et amplius, et prefata Margareta est etatis unius anni et amplius. Et dicunt quod predictus Henricus nullas alias terras sen tenementa tenuit dicto die quo obiit in comitatu predicto in dominico aut in servicio de dicto Domino Rege nec de aliquo alio. In cujus rei testimonium huic inquisicioni jurati predicti sigilla sua apposuerunt. Data die loco et anno supradictis.

---

*Record Office, Tower of London.*

*Inquisitio post mortem, 7th Henry V.—No.* 21.

Inquisicio capta apud Wolvernehamptone 10^o· die mensis Januarij anno regni Regis Henrici quinti post conquestum septimo coram Willielmo Lee Escaetore Domini Regis in comitatu Staffordie . . . . . . . per sacramentum Thome Corbyn, Thome del Hoo, Willielmi del Mersshe, Rogeri Hankys, Willielmi Rous, Johannis Walstevode, Willielmi Lydeyate, Ricardi Hykeson, Thome Swetcoke, Thome Brereley, Roberti Ays-

sheley et Willielmi Bernesley qui dicunt . . . . quod Alicia filia
Henrici Hervyle in dicto brevi nominata tenuit in dominico suo ut de
feodo, die quo habitum religionis assumsit in quo professa est, terciam
partem manerii de Wednesbury cum pertinenciis in comitatu Staffordie. .
. . . Item tenuit terciam partem manerii de Tynmore . . . et
terciam partem xl acrarum terre etc. . . . . . in Tibyntone. . .
Et dicunt quod predicta Alicia professa fuit in Festo Sancte Trinitatis jam
ultimo preterito. Et quod Johanna uxor Willielmi Leventhorpe est soror
et heres predicte Alicie propinquior. Et est etatis xvii annorum et amplius.
In cujus rei etc.—(Abstract only.)

[A precisely similar inquisition on Margaret, the other daughter of Henry Hervyle.
She also being described as "Etatis xvii. annorum et amplius," and Joan, the wife of
William Leventhorpe, her sister and nearest heir.]

————

Record Office, Tower of London,
          Inquisitio post mortem 12th Edward IV. No. 32.

Inquisicio capta apud Wyllenhale 28°· Junij anno Edwardi IV. duodecimo
per sacramentum Jacobi Levesone arm! Cornelij Wyrley, arm. , Rici
Levesone arm! , Radulphi Busshbury armigeri, Rob. Levesone, Willi.
Mollesley, Willi. Colborne, Johīs Lutteley, Henrici Walstewode, Johīs
Clerke, Willi. Robyns et Thome Duddeley qui dicunt super sacramentum
suum quod Henricus Beaumont miles non tenuit aliquas terras tenementa
etc. die quo obiit sed dicunt quod quidam Johannes Hampton de Stourton
armiger fuit seisitus in dominico suo—de Manerio de Wednesbury—et
terris in Typton ad usum predicti Henrici—et Alianore uxoris ejus—et
inde seisitus per quandam cartam suam—dedit et concessit prefate Alianore
nuper uxori predicti Henrici Beaumont in brevi nominati predictum
Manerium de Wednesbury etc. Habendum et tenendum predicte Alianore
ad terminum vite sue . . . et quod post decessum ipsius Alianore
manerium predictum etc. remaneant in perpetuum heredibus inter prefatum
Henr. Beaumont—et dictam Alianoram nuper uxorem suam—

Quod predicta Alianora nuper uxor predicti Henrici superstes—in plena
vita existit—

Quod idem Henricus obiit 16 Novembris anno regni Regis predicti
undecimo. Et quod Johannes Beaumont est filius et heres predicti Henrici
propinquior et etatis duorum annorum et amplius. In cujus etc., etc.—
(Abstract only.)

is
le
n
·
t
1
r
·
·
;

40.

Alianor.

on.——Juliana.   Living 1325.
   ╆╆

ne.

ter and heir of John de Tynmore.

ghter and heir of William Sperner.

William L    Margareta, 3rd daughter, æt. 1, 1406.   Became
                a Nun 1420.

d heir.

Sister of John Lord Dudley, afterwards wife of
   George Stanley.

John                    James Beaumont.——Elizabeth,
2,                                            ╆╆

William Babh m fry Babington, of Rothley,——Elianor, 3rd daughter.
   county of Leicester.                        ╆╆

# CHAPTER II.

## The Parish Church.

---

**O**ur Saxon predecessors, as early as the eighth century, erected their buildings after the style of the Romans, taking as their example the decaying edifices which the latter had built during their occupation of England. At that period, and even down to the twelfth century, architecture was but little developed. The Roman, the Saxon, and the Norman styles, gradually succeeded one another, each possessing its own distinctive peculiarities—the two latter originating from the former. Subsequently England produced a style, inferior to none in purity of Gothic principle, and surpassing every other in the matchless beauty of its detail.* This style—the Early English—may well be the pride of Englishmen; for not only is it almost exclusively our own, but it has produced a train of cathedrals, abbeys, and other churches, the most glorious which our land can boast. Almost nine-tenths of our most magnificent churches owe their chiefest beauties to this style, and, with whatever other variety of Pointed architecture it is brought in contact, its merits shine forth

* Freeman.

preeminently, and, so far from suffering, gains additional
lustre by the comparison.*   Probably, after this elegant
style the first church, erected on the ruins of Ethelfleda's
Castle, was built and proportioned.   The precise date of its
erection, however, cannot with any degree of certainty be
fixed; but, from the absence of any mention of a church in
Doomsday Book,—whilst the neighbouring parishes of Wolverhampton, Sedgley, Alrewas, Pattingham, Brewood, Lichfield, and Stafford, and several others, are recorded as
possessing churches, with resident incumbents,—it may be
possible that Wednesbury had not one at that period; still
it is not decisive evidence that there was not then a church,
as we find whole counties without any notice of the churches.

The first mention of the existence of a church, that we
are able to discover, is during the reign of King John, who
presented one of his chaplains to the living of Wednesbury,
and, also, one to Walsall.   The church, therefore, was most
probably built between the years 1080 and 1216.

This church afterwards belonged to the Abbot and Convent
of Hales Owen, who grounded their right of patronage to it
upon a charter of King Henry III., whereby the church of
Walsall, and its chapels of Wednesbury and Rushall, were
given to that abbey for ever.†   This right they enjoyed un-
disturbed until the twenty-first year of Edward I., (A.D.
1293), when a " *quo warranto* "‡ was issued, by the crown,
against the Abbot of Hales Owen, for the recovery of the
advowson of Wednesbury.   The case was tried before John
de Berwick and his associates, itinerating justices of the
county of Stafford.

The king founded his title upon the fact that the advowson
formerly belonged to the crown, in the time of King John,

---

* Scott's Plea for the Faithful Restoration of Ancient Churches.
  † Appendix B.                ‡ Appendix C.

who presented one of his chaplains to the living, as before mentioned, and, consequently, the right of presentation descended to the reigning monarch.

The Abbot defended his right, " pleading the charter of Henry III., the father of Edward I., whereby the church of Walsall, with its chapels of Wednesbury and Rushall, were granted to the abbey of Hales Owen for ever."

Hugo de Lowther, however, on the part of the crown, " contended that at the time of King Henry's grant, the church of Wednesbury was *not* one of the chapels belonging to Walsall, but had, for some time previously, been a mother church, and was in no way connected with Walsall." In support of his plea he brought forward as witnesses, among others, William de Wrotteslegh and John Heronville; so verdict was given for the king, and the crown recovered the advowson. The same year in which this cause was tried the king accepted a fine of ten marks from the Abbot, and by a deed, bearing date 1301,* the right of presentation, together with the tithes and other emoluments, were given up by the crown to the abbey of Hales Owen for ever, and they were further secured by a grant from the Bishop of Coventry and Lichfield, (A.D. 1305),† by virtue whereof the abbey regained the possession of the advowson; nevertheless, after this, instances occur of the vicar being appointed still by the crown. At the time of the dissolution of monasteries, between 1535—9, King Henry VIII. gave to Sir John Dudley, Knight, to be held in military tenure, the rectories of Clent, Wednesbury, and Walsall.

It is somewhat strange that the first grant of the church of Walsall, with its chapels, to the aforesaid abbey, was made by Sir William Rous, or Rufus, as appears from a deed

* Appendix D.     † Appendix E.

E

recorded in the "Monasticon;"* but, notwithstanding this, the Abbot obtained a fresh grant from King Henry III. from whence it would appear that he was cognizant of a previous claim of the crown thereto, which induced him to take this step; and being then possessed of the advowson, he next obtained the appropriation of the tithes, by license from the bishop. It was thus that Walsall was constituted a *vicarage*.

The probable time when the church of Wednesbury was first erected has been already stated; but it appears afterwards to have undergone a thorough repair, about the latter half of the fifteenth century, when the style of architecture predominant at that period, viz., the Perpendicular, was visible throughout; and it may be interesting to specify in this place the original dimensions of the church,† as existing before the late alterations in 1828: they were as follows :—

|                          | ft. | in. |
|--------------------------|-----|-----|
| Chancel—length           | 42  | 0   |
| „        breadth         | 21  | 0   |
| Nave—length              | 50  | 4   |
| „      breadth           | 21  | 0   |
| South aisle—breadth      | 17  | 8   |
| North „        „         | 19  | 8   |

Both aisles were of the same length as the nave. On the east side of the south aisle was a chapel separated by arches from the other part of the building, and a part of it, about one half, was afterwards partitioned off for a vestry. At the entrance to the chancel there stood an organ, which was destroyed by the soldiery of Oliver Cromwell, the effects of whose fanatical and sacrilegious rage are seen more or less in many of our beautiful cathedrals and parish churches.

* Appendix F.
† Shaw's History of Staffordshire.

THE LECTERN.
SCALE ONE INCH TO THE FOOT.

In the chancel were fifteen stalls of curious workmanship, beautifully carved, of various designs, and bearing the usual characteristics of the Perpendicular style of architecture. Many interesting monuments now remain there, to the memory of the Parkes (ancestors of Lord Ward), Harcourts, Hopkins, Comberfords, and others. The communion rails bore the date 1686, legibly inscribed thereon. The oaken pulpit exhibits the date 1611. The windows were richly adorned with much stained glass, bearing among other devices, the arms of Heronville, Beaumont, Comberford, Babington, and others.* The eagle lectern deserves particular notice, as well on account of its antiquity, as of the purpose for which it was designed—the use of it being much more ancient than that of the pulpit.† The original high-pitched roof was afterwards superseded by one in the Tudor style, of a more obtuse form—the pitch of which was much lower, and even approached to flatness. It consisted of numerous rectangular compartments, formed by the intersection of the timbers ; and these compartments were subdivided by moulded ribs, which were ornamented with carved bosses, painted and gilt. The chancel roof was supported, or appeared to be, by carved figures of priests, in albs ; one bearing a shield, another a dulcimer, another a trumpet, and a fourth a drum, besides others too much decayed to be described. The porch is plain, but of the same style of architecture as the chancel. It is thickly coated with cement and plaster, which prevent much of its details being seen. The arch at the entrance is segmental, and exhibits the mouldings carried up from the base to the spring ; and hence, without the interposition of any capital, in a continuous sweep to its apex. The windows—one on each side—are

* Appendix G.     † Appendix H.

each divided into two compartments, and are also segmental, within a square head—of which examples in this style are far from common. The roof is divided into eight cellular compartments ; at the intersection of the ribs the bosses are carved—the centre one bearing the sacred monogram— I. H. S. The porch was formerly a favourite place of sepulture, but is now chiefly occupied by the vault of the Haden family.

At the entrance into the churchyard the lych gate formerly stood, affording a convenient shelter, where the corpse might rest, as directed by the Rubric, until the arrival of the cler, gyman. It is, in our opinion, unfortunate that this lych gate has been destroyed, as there are so few remaining in the county.

Cooke states* that, " about sixty years ago, the walls in the inside of the church were ornamented with paintings by some masterly pencil, and which might have continued many years to come, had not the sacrilegious hand of a common mason, with a whitewashing brush, put a final end to their beauty."

From a document that was found in the roof of the church, during the late somewhat partial restoration, we learn that the church was repaired in the year 1766. The workmen employed received two shillings per day. This was during the incumbency of the Rev. Edward Best. In lapse of time the church had greatly fallen into decay. The Rev. John Atcherley, the curate, in a published letter† complains "that the pulpit had literally streamed with rain whilst he stood there, and that he was frequently exposed to the rude attacks of winter, when engaged in the service of the Church. The churchyard wall was partly in ruins, and, indeed, the whole

---

* Topographical Library of Great Britain.          † A.D. 1805.

fabric seemed likely to perish." If, however, the guardians
of the church, in days gone by, had neglected their duty,
yet, at a later period, they were more alive to their respon-
sibilities, for in 1828, the church was partially restored and
enlarged; but, unfortunately owing to the degenerate state of
art, no attention was paid to its fair proportions and elegant
workmanship, so that its *individual* character—whereby it
was distinguished in common with other parish churches,
from those of neighbouring places—was completely lost, and
its *traditional* character wholly obliterated. And here we
would express our conviction, that those to whom the con-
servation and restoration of such buildings are committed
" should exercise their duties with a reverential care, lest,
while restoring them to a state of seemly reparation, they
efface or alter their details—lest, while repairing the casket,
the jewel it contains be lost; a jewel not handed for *our* use
only, but given us in trust, that we may transmit it to generations having more knowledge and more skill to use it
aright. Nearly every restorer has his favourite style or some
fancy notion to which he wishes to make everything subservient; and it is a most lamentable fact that there has been
far more done to obliterate genuine examples of Pointed
architecture, by the tampering caprices of *well-meant* restora-
tions, than had been effected by centuries of mutilation and
neglect. A restored church appears to lose all its truthful-
ness, and to become as little authentic, as an example of
ancient art, as if it had been rebuilt on a new design. The
restorer too often preserves *only* just what he fancies, and
alters even that if it is not quite in accordance with his taste.
*The practical workman detests restoration,* and will always
*destroy* and *renew* rather than *preserve* and *restore*, so that an
antagonistic influence ought always to be at hand. When
any of the ancient seats or other woodwork remain, they

ought to be carefully preserved and repaired, though perhaps rough and plain. The same remarks apply to encaustic tiles, fragments of stained glass, or ancient ironwork, and their patterns should be generally followed, although it is possible that finer examples might be found elsewhere."* We could have desired that this *conservative* principle had been carried out in the late restoration of our noble parish church, but unfortunately it was totally disregarded. The elegant chancel was shortened by the nave being carried out towards it; and at its entrance was placed a pile of timber, called a "reading desk," and "clerk's desk," surmounted by the ancient pulpit,† (removed from its former position), which serves effectually to hide the Communion Table, the Creed, the Lord's Prayer, and the Ten Commandments, from the view of a great portion of the congregation. The stalls were nearly all demolished, none of them being suffered to remain in the chancel or in the church, but became the property of the builder, who allowed them to be conveyed away. The other carved work shared the same fate, being actually wheeled away in barrows, to be converted into articles of domestic use, or whatever else the spoliator might think fit. Thus, the curiously wrought back of a seat, or part of a screen, was seen doing duty as a shutter to an upper window of a mean house in the town; whilst, on the opposite side of the way, the stable door of a public house bore the sacred monogram and fleur-de-lis, being part of the spoils of the roof of the parish church. The windows, likewise, suffered much at different periods, so that now only a very small portion of the original glass remains, consisting of some few fragments to be seen in the vestry. This is greatly to be regretted, as they contained, in heraldic devices, much of the

* Scott's Plea, &c.
† Such a pile has been wittily termed a *three-decker*.

history of the lords of the manor. The porch and spire, with a peal of eight bells, remain as formerly. The church, as enlarged, consists of a nave, two aisles, with spacious galleries, a chapel on the south side, with a building, intended to correspond, on the north, and contains 1300 sittings, of which 459 are free and unappropriated. It was re-opened on Sunday, November 9, 1828, when, after sermons preached, in the morning by the Rev. A. B. Haden,* jun., and in the evening by the Lord Bishop of the Diocese,† £174 were collected, and, on the following day, a further sum of £114 was added, after a musical service. The entire cost of re-building was about £5500. The sum of £500 was given by the Incorporated Society for Building Churches and Chapels; £1500 were borrowed, to be repaid in ten years by church rates; and the remainder was raised by private sub-scriptions and the sale of pews. The present chancel windows were presented by the late Samuel Addison, Esq. They are filled with stained glass, the centre one bearing the figure of S. Bartholomew, to whom the church is dedi-cated, but is inferior in design and execution. The fine toned organ (not occupying the position of its ancient prede-cessor), which cost £500, was the gift of Benjamin Wright, Esq., of Birmingham, A.D. 1830, in remembrance of his native place, and in lieu of the one presented in the year 1807 by the late Rev. John Rose Holden. Under the com-munion table is an incised monumental slab,‡ bearing the effigies of Richard Jennyns and Isabel his wife, with the following inscription :—

Of your charytie praye for the soules of Richard Jennyns and Isabel his wyfe, the which Richard departed . . . . M̄DXXX, being LXXVIII yeares of age, of whose soules Jesus have mercy. Amen.

* Now Vicar of Brewood. † Dr. Henry Ryder.

‡ This slab is marked with five small crosses, which is a singular and interesting example of an usage now and then seen of marking a monumental stone with the same sacred emblems as was formerly done upon stone altars.

Within the chancel rails is a monumental slab bearing the figures of a man in armour, and also the effigy of a lady, and one son and four daughters at their feet, with this marginal inscription :—

Of your charyte praye for the soule of Jhon Cumberfort, Gentylman, and Em' hys wyffe, the whyche Jhon departed the xxb day of Aperyll in the yere of oure Lord God MD LIX, of whose soule God have mercy.

There are also, within the rails, on an alabaster monument, two recumbent figures, with the following inscription at the feet :—

Christicolis colamenque suis Solamen egenis,
Patronime studiis nunc lapis iste tegit.

On the front, at top :—

Μακαριοι οἱ νεκροι ἐν Κυριῳ ἀποθνησκοντες, ἀπαρτ.

To number our days so teach us that we may apply our hearts unto wisdom.—*Psalm* 90, *v.* 12.—[In the Hebrew character.]

In the middle :—

This sad monument
Sheweth the body of that worthy, generous,
and general labourer, (much wanted
and lamented,) Richard Parkes,
Esquire, onlye sonne of that
well deserving father T. Parkes,
deceased, whome God called
to mercy, May vii. MDCXVIII.
anno ætatis LV.
Intom'b here lyes our dearest friend belowe,
Whom Love and Hope entombs our hapless woe ;
All knew his heart, and art, and hand, still bent
To countrey, Church, to friends, to poor's lamente,
Too soone tho' lay'd within this earthly wombe,
His living deeds shall make our hearts his tombe.
Ερχου Κυριε Ιησου.

At the head :—

> Τῆς ἀρετῆς φίλον, φρόνιμον, φιλοπάτριδα κοινον
> Τοις ἀγαθον πασιν, ὃν τάφος ὀυτος ἔχει.

On the chancel floor, on the north side, there is a small stone thus inscribed :—" Nov. xxiii, 1672, M.H.," with the arms, in a lozenge-shaped shield, of the Hopkins family.

There originally stood against the north wall an ancient monument, rudely sculptured, with two female figures, standing under Gothic niches, each resting the right hand on a plain shield, with no inscription.* On the south wall is another—a man and woman kneeling, and under them six children, viz:—three sons (whereof one is in a cradle) and three daughters :—

> To the memory of his countrey's lover, churche's beautifier, and poor's benefactor, Thomas Parkes, gent. and Elianor his wife, which Thomas deceased Jan. xvii, 1602, anno æt. lxx.

> Ingressum vitæ dat mors finemque labori,
> Vivere cum Christo quam mihi dulce mori !

> Bodies lye breathless, souls to Heaven ascend,
> Then come Death deathless, Joy's gate, Sorrow's end.

> Justorum animæ in manu Dei sunt;
> Requiescunt a laboribus suis, & opera illorum
> Sequuntur illos.

> Πῦ σε θάνατε τὸ κέντρον, πῦ σε ἀδη, τὸ νίκος;

On the west wall of the south transept, on a marble tablet, is the following :—

> In cujus beneficii perrennem memoriam Franciscus Wortleius de Wortley Ebor. miles et baron, (quondam patronus suus) hanc commemorationem illi servorumque fidelitate dicavit. Hic a cunabilis Marti dicatus nil nisi inhonestum non ausus, ardua gressus, san- ͟

* Shaw's History of Staffordshire.

F

guinem sudoremque perpessus.  In juventute veteranus, in arte
militari peritus inter cohortes regi Persarum assignatas centurio
electus, jam iter facturus in matrem pietate ardens Ithacam petijt,
febri maligna insidiatus, Persarum arma deposuit, Christi induit,
solita magnanimitate, insolita alacritate animæ aromata cum hisce
verbis (euge bone fidelisque serve) suaviter exhalavit : sic invictus
cecidit non perijt 1636.

There was also at the foot, below the altar rails, near
where this monument formerly stood :—

Hic jacet Gualterus Hercourte, stemmate pernobilis, virtute nobiliori
qui Dominum suum assassinatorum gladiis obsessum stupenda
magnanimitate (etiam in pueritia) munivit et liberavit.*

Above the former inscription are the following arms :—

1. Gules, 2 barrs Or.
2. Azure, 3 lions passant Argent.
3. Or, a frett Gules, a canton Argent.
4. Barry undy Argent and Gules, a bordure bésantée.
5. Azure, a sun in its full glory.
6. Argent, a lion rampant Sable.
7. Sable, fretty Or.
8. Argent, a lion rampant Vert.
9. Barry of eight pieces Or and Gules.
10. Per pale Or and Vert, a cross patoncè Gules.
11. Gules, a chevron Argent, between ten besants Or.
12. Vert, a fess between three lions heads cabosed.
13. Vert, a chief Gules, a lion rampant double queved Argent.
14. Vert, three spread eagles Sable.
15. Vert, a bend between six cross croslets.
16. Argent, on a chief Gules, two stags heads cabosed.
17. Argent, on a fess Gules, three billets Or.
18. Gules, on a bend wavy three ducks Sable.
19. Argent, a fess, between three boars heads cabosed Sable, tusked Or·
20. Argent, a chevron engrailed Gules, between three bugle horns Vert·
     stringed of the second.
     Crest, on a helmet crowned Or, a peacock.†

* Shaw's History of Staffordshire.  This is now lost.        † Ibid.

The undermentioned monuments are also to be found in various parts of the church, viz. :—

At the west end, near the font :—

Sacred to the memory of Elizabeth, the wife of George Watkins, of this town, who closed an invaluable life on the 21st of July, 1791, aged 54 years, sincerely regretted by her numerous friends and by her surviving relations.

Also of the above George Watkins, who, on the 7th day of January, 1810, in the 80th year of his age, terminated a life distinguished by unaffected piety, parental affection, extensive charity, and unreserved benevolence.

At the west end of the north aisle :—

Underneath are deposited the remains of Thomas Rowlinson, late of this town, potter, who, by will, dated the 19th of September, 1821, left one hundred pounds to the churchwardens for the time being, in trust, to invest in Government or real securities, at interest, and to apply and expend such interest in the purchase of bread, to be distributed amongst such poor persons, inhabitants of the parish of Wednesbury, as they shall think proper, on Good Friday, yearly for ever. He departed this life the 11th of July, 1824, aged 76 years.

In the north aisle, near the porch :—

Sacred to the memory of Joseph Hobson, who departed this life March 6, 1802, aged 55 years. Likewise of Elizabeth, wife of the above. She departed this life November 11th, 1817, aged 67 years.

At the east end of the north aisle :—

Sacred to the memory of Samuel Addison, Esq., banker; born at Charnes, in this county, July 21st, 1766 ; commenced business as a grocer, in Wednesbury, 1786 ; died May 8, 1849, in the 83rd year of his age, having survived his wife and three sons. As a banker for nearly half a century in this town, he was cautious, considerate, successful; as a magistrate, he was impartial, patient,

just; as a citizen, he was loyal, courteous, upright. He greatly
aided the rebuilding of this church, 1828. He gave the site for S.
John's Church, and five hundred pounds to the building fund, 1846.
A few weeks before his death he contracted for the erection of the
spire, at a cost of seven hundred pounds, and by his will bequeathed
to the poor of this parish three thousand pounds. This tablet is
erected by his executors as a memorial of his industry and
perseverance.

Soli Deo Gloria.

## In the chancel, on the north wall :—

In memory of Mary, the beloved and lamented wife of Samuel Addison,
who died November 12, 1796, aged 24 years. Also of William,
their son, who died May 13, 1796, aged 8 months. Likewise of
Samuel, their eldest son, who died June 20, 1817, aged 24 years
beloved by his friends, and esteemed by all who knew him. Also of
their last surviving son, John Addison, Esq., banker, of this town,
who died March 29th, 1840, aged 45 years. In relative, social,
and public life, he was all a father could desire, a most affectionate
and dutiful son, a warm and sincere friend, a useful and exemplary
member of society, an active, impartial, and faithful magistrate. For
several years he filled the office of churchwarden of this parish with
zeal, tempered with discretion, and was mainly instrumental, in the
year 1829, in the rebuilding and enlarging of this church—in a
vault on the north side of which his mortal remains are deposited
with those of his beloved mother and brothers, in sure and certain
hope of the resurrection to eternal life, through Jesus Christ our
only Lord and Saviour. The father, who has survived his wife and
all their children, in sorrow, erects this monument.

## Inside the altar rails, north side :—

In memory of the Rev. Alexander Bunn Haden, B.A., vicar of this
parish 48 years, and in the commission of the peace of Stafford
and Salop, who, greatly beloved and lamented, died May 13th, 1829,
aged 77 years. Also of Mary Haden, his wife, who died June 22nd,
1837, aged 86 years.

I know that my Redeemer liveth.

On the north side of the altar, inside the rails :—

As a memorial of Edward Crowther, Esquire, who departed this life
the 18th of January, 1822, aged 48 years, and Stephen Faulkner
Crowther, Esquire, on the 26th of December, 1829, aged 52
years, whose remains are deposited in the family vault at Claverley,
in Shropshire, and who practised in partnership as solicitors in this
town, and during a long professional career were distinguished for
sound judgment, great industry, benevolence, and undeviating integ-
rity. This tablet is erected expressive of their virtues, in the midst
of the scene of their usefulness, by their only surviving brother, John
Crowther, the last branch of the family.

On the north chancel wall, outside the rails :—

In a vault, near this spot, are deposited the remains of William Holden,
late of Birmingham, in the county of Warwick, merchant, who
departed this life April 9th, 1806, in the 89th year of his age.
Also of Mary, his wife, third daughter of John Rose, of Daventry,
in the county of Northampton, gent., who died in September, 1752.
Also of John Rose Holden, M.A., clerk, eldest son of the above
William and Mary Holden, late of Summer Hill, Birmingham,
patron, and some time rector of Upminster, in the county of Essex,
who died January 28th, 1827, in the 77th year of his age. Also
of Mary, wife of the above John Rose Holden, daughter of William
Tovey, of Eardington, in the county of Warwick, gent., who died
December 9th, 1829, in the 82nd year of her age.

On the floor, partly hidden by the monument to the
Addison family, and in many parts wholly illegible, is a
stone, with the following inscription :—

 . . . . . . . . . Millerdi
Hujus ecclesiæ vicarii
vir ingenio . . . . . . . .
. . . . . . . . ab omnibus admirandâ
Hic requiescit in spe
beatæ resurrectionis
Obiit duodecimo die Nobris anno Dom. MDCLxxxviii.

Between the monuments of Richard Parkes and Thomas
Parkes, on the south chancel wall :—

> In remembrance of the late Philip Williams, of Wednesbury Oak Iron
> Works, this tablet, a poor and inadequate memorial of his many social
> and domestic virtues, is erected by his grateful and affectionate
> family. His diligence and perseverance under God's blessing pro-
> cured him affluence, whilst by his vigour and capacity, united with
> liberal and enlarged views, he was enabled to develope the resources
> of the iron trade, and not only to benefit this neighbourhood, but to
> further the prosperity of his country. He lived honoured and
> beloved, and died in humble reliance on the merits of his Saviour,
> on the 19th of January, 1829, in the 54th year of his age. Also of
> Ann, wife of the above-named Philip Williams, who departed this life
> on the 7th of October, 1808, aged 34 years. Also of Elizabeth,
> second wife of the above-named Philip Williams, who departed this
> life on the 31st of January, 1821, aged 47 years. Also of James,
> son of Philip and Ann Williams, who departed this life on the 30th
> of September, 1836, aged 35 years. Also of Thomas, son of Philip
> and Ann Williams, who departed this life on the 11th of October,
> 1839, aged 39 years.

At the east end of the south aisle :—

> In memory of Frederick Lees, son of William and Jane Lees, of this
> parish, surgeon, who departed this life December 22, 1844, aged
> 37 years. His amiable and ingenuous disposition deeply endeared
> him to his family and friends, while his unremitting assiduity and
> kindness in his profession attracted universal esteem. His surviving
> brothers and sisters have erected this tablet in token of their affec-
> tionate remembrance.

> In affectionate remembrance of Benjamin Brown, who departed this
> life January 15th, 1844, aged 68 years, whose kind and benevolent
> disposition deservedly endeared him to his family and friends.

In the south aisle, near the former :—

> John Hodgkins, dyed October 21, A.D. 1779, æ. 69 years. Eliz., his
> wife, dyed September 21st, A.D. 1781, æ. 88 years.

Near the middle of the south aisle :—

Sacred to the memory of Francis Wastie Haden, Esq., Deputy Commissary General, second son of the Rev. A. B. Haden, vicar of this parish. He served first in the army under the command of his Grace the Duke of Wellington during the whole of the Peninsular war, in the later years of which offices of high trust and responsibility were confided to him. He was next employed as chief of the Commissariat at the British Settlement of Nova Scotia, from whence, after seven years' service, he was transferred, with the same appointment, to the Garrison of Gibraltar; there his duties ceased with his life, on the 13th day of March, 1828, in the 43rd year of his age. His talents and unwearied zeal in the discharge of his various professional duties obtained for him the warmest testimonies of approbation and the entire confidence of his superiors, by whom his services were pronounced to be important and advantageous to his country; but it is chiefly to record his private worth that those who knew him best, and therefore loved him most, have erected this monument; and while they deplore his early removal, lamenting his loss as an exemplary husband, father, son, and brother, they derive solace from the remembrance of his piety and other Christian virtues—virtues which shed happiness and reflected honour on his own family, and received their appropriate earthly recompense in the affectionate regard of all who knew him.

Near the south porch are the following :—

Sacred to the memory of Thomas Watkins Yardley, who died December 9th, 1840, in the 30th year of his age.

Sacred to the memory of John Jesson, of Walsall, who died the 24th of December, 1774, aged 41. Also Ann, his wife, died the 5th of May, 1763, aged 30. Also John, their son, who died the 27th of November, 1782, aged 26. Also Ann, their daughter, died young, whose remains are interred underneath this seat.

The remaining monuments in the church are upon the floor, and are as follows :—

To the memory of Hyla Holden, Esq. Ob. 12 Nov., 1810.

In memory of Joseph Babb, gent., of Stratford, Essex, who departed this life July 21, 1772, aged 70. Also in memory of Elizabeth Babb, his wife, who died January 1, 1801, 96th year of her age.

Near this place lie the remains of Samuel Humphreys, who died June 15th, 1805, aged 71 years.

In memory of Thomas Sanders . . . . . . . . . . . 1739, aged . . . . . . . . . .

John Cox, died February 4, 1729, aged 7 months.

Joseph Wood, dyed August 12th, 1728, aged 7 months.

John Cox Wood, dyed May 9th, 1731, aged 1 year and 6 months.

John Cox Wood and Mary, dyed ye 7 & ye 24 April, 1733, aged 6 months —being children of Joseph and Mary Wood, his wife.

Henry Wood, dyed November 5th, 1760, aged 36 years.

Also James Wood, who died September 5th, 1813, aged 36 years. Turn again, then, unto thy rest, O my soul, for the Lord hath rewarded thee.

There are several other monumental slabs in the church, but the inscriptions are not legible.

In concluding this chapter, we would observe, that in the remarks we have before made, we do not undervalue the respect which the inhabitants of Wednesbury have shewn for their parish church. That is not our object. We would fain confess that the *motive* which induced the attempted restoration was noble and praiseworthy, and we regret to be obliged to speak at all disparagingly of the *manner* in which it was effected. But we venture to express our earnest hope, that the Mother Church of the parish may eventually be restored to her former beautiful proportions, and again be the pride and admiration of the inhabitants.

# CHAPTER III.

## The Vicars.

---

After dioceses were divided into parishes, the secular clergy, who had the charge in those parishes, were called rectors; but when the benefices were appropriated to religious houses, " the great tithes were reserved for the abbey-fund, and the small tithes left as a miserable stipend (often not more than the sixteenth part of the revenue of the benefice) to the minister, who took the monk's labouring oar, under the title of " *vicarius*." Thus Wednesbury, upon being given to the Abbot and Convent of Hales Owen, became a vicarage. So " it came to pass that town livings (contrary to all reason) are at present, of all others, the poorest—less than the usual pittance having been left them by the *considerate* monks, who reckoned, and, perhaps, wisely reckoned, in the days when Masses were said, that a large population would supply by free alms an adequate provision for the vicar."*

* Blunt's Sketch of the Reformation.

G

The following account of the Vicars of Wednesbury is not so full and complete as could have been desired; but when the length of time between the first institution to the vicarage here recorded, and the date of the admission of the present incumbent, is taken into consideration, (a space of at least 600 years,) it will at once be seen that a correct and perfect list could hardly be expected. Under such circumstances, it is considered advisable to supply the best that could be obtained, with the hope that the names now given of those who have succeeded each other as ministers of the church, in this ancient parish, will not be uninteresting.

| DATE OF INSTITUTION. | VICARS. | PATRONS. |
|---|---|---|
| Between 1199 and 1216 | William | King John. |
| March 4, 1293 | Nicholaus de Burtone | Edward I. |

Upon the king giving up his right to the patronage A.D. 1301, he resigned in favour of his successor, on condition that the Abbot and Convent of Hales Owen paid him ten marks annually.—See Appendix D.

| | | |
|---|---|---|
| June 1 or 2, 1301 | Thomas de Hales | { Abbot and Convent of Hales Owen. |
| May 18, 1448 | Johannes Brounfield | Henry VI. |
| Before 1534 | Richard Jenyns | |
| April 19, 1547 | Thomas Baynes | The Crown. |
| October 6, 1548 | William Starismore | The Crown. |
| Before 1553 | Richard Jenyns | |

It appears, says Shaw, from an old deed, that amongst the pensions paid in 1553 to incumbents of chantries, he received £2 14s. 4d. as incumbent.

| | | |
|---|---|---|
| 1553 | Edmund Walker | The Crown. |
| Before 1561 | Richard Dolphin | |

He was buried at Wednesbury, March 28, 1619.

| | | |
|---|---|---|
| April 17, 1619 | Richard Dolphin | The Crown. |
| Before 1662 | William Fincher | |

He resigned on S. Bartholomew's Day, 1662.

| | | |
|---|---|---|
| June 16, 1663 | John Torbuck | The Crown |
| November 23, 1664 | William Millar | The Crown |

Buried at Wednesbury, November 16, 1688.

| | | |
|---|---|---|
| May 7, 1689 | Thomas Oakes | The Crown. |

| DATE OF INSTITUTION. | VICARS. | PATRONS. |
|---|---|---|
| April 8, 1693 | Francis Williams | The Crown. |
| March 26, 1707 | Edward Best | The Crown. |
| 1719 | Edward Egginton | The Crown. |
| 1743 | Edward Best | The Crown. |

Buried at Wednesbury, July 12, 1782, aged 74 years.

| | | |
|---|---|---|
| July 25, 1782 | Alexander Bunn Haden | The Crown. |
| August 8, 1829 | Isaac Clarkson | The Crown. |

The following is a list of the Curates of the Parish Church, as far as they have been ascertained:—

| DATE. | NAME. | DATE. | NAME. |
|---|---|---|---|
| 1471 | John Twycrosse. | 1805 | John Atcherly. |
| 1500 | William Jenyns. | 1805 | Charles Neve. |
| As appears from the Rent Roll of Hales Owen Abbey. | | —— | John Loyd. |
| 1540 | William Turner. | —— | ——Marsden. |
| 1698 | Richard Allen. | —— | William Tate. |
| 1699 | Thomas Thomas. | 1821—June 1 | Isaac Clarkson. |
| 1700 | Edward Best. | 1831—2 | William Hunt. |
| Afterwards Vicar. | | —— | J R. Hore. |
| 1727 | George Hancock. | —— | W. H. Marychurch |
| 1728 | William Weate. | —— | J. T. D. Kidd. |
| 1744 | —— Wright. | —— | Thomas Dawes. |
| 1746 | —— Roe. | —— | Richard Goldham. |
| 1761—3 | —— Dallaway. | —— | J. H. Broome. |
| 1764 | —— Parry. | —— | Joseph Hall. |
| 1765 | —— Lloyd. | —— | Charles Churton. |
| 1770 | Littelton Perry. | 1853 | C. H. Coleman. |
| —— | J. Palmer. | —— | Henry Taylor, |
| | | Assistant Curate for King's Hill and Delves. | |

Curates of Moxley :—

| | |
|---|---|
| H. B. Mason. | John Winter. |
| J. F. Fanshawe. | Thomas Knight. |

The living, as we have already stated, is in the gift of the Crown, and is a discharged vicarage, valued in the

King's Book at £4 3s. 4d. It is estimated at the present time to be worth £310 per annum.

The following document will shew the apportionment of the rent charge in lieu of tithe:—

**Now** I, John George Weddall, of North Hall, near Howden, in the east riding of the county of York, having been duly appointed valuer, to apportion the total sum awarded to be paid by way of rent charge, in lieu of tithes, amongst the several lands of the said parish of Wednesbury, do hereby apportion the rent charge as follows:—

Gross rent charge, payable to the tithe owners in lieu of tithes, for the parish of Wednesbury, in the county of Stafford, four hundred and eighty pounds, viz:—

|  | £ |
|---|---|
| To the Vicar | 220 |
| „  „ Earl of Dartmouth | 10 |
| „  „ Vicar of Dudley | 10 |
| „ Nathaniel Phillips | 5 |
| „ Sir Edward Dolman Scott and Edward Thomas Foley, Esq. | 235 |
|  | £480 |

Value in imperial bushels and decimal parts of an imperial bushel of wheat, barley, and oats.

|  | Price per Bushel. | | Bushels and Decimal parts. |
|---|---|---|---|
|  | s. | d. | |
| Wheat | 7 | 0¼ | 455,78635 |
| Barley | 3 | 11¼ | 808,42105 |
| Oats | 2 | 9 | 1163,63686 |

We subjoin the following extracts from the *Registry of the Bishop of Lichfield*, relating to Wednesbury and Walsall, and also the terriers of 1612 and 1726, from the same registry:—

*Extracted from the Registry of the Bishop of Lichfield.*

*Episcopal Register, No.* 1, *p.* 42 —1309, *June* 10.

Memorandum quod iv<sup>to.</sup> Idus Junii anno Domini 1309 Frater Thomas de Hales Abbathie de Hales canonicus et presbiter admissus fuit apud London ad vicariam de Waleshale tunc vacantem per mortem Fratris Galfridi ultimi vicarii ejusdem, et incepit vacare die Mercurii in vigilia Apostolorum Philippi et Jacobi. Et institutus fuit canonice in eadem ad presentacionem religiosorum virorum Abbatis et Conventus de Hales. Et mandabatur Archdiacono vel ejus officiali quod induceret eum in corporalem possessionem. Sub eadem data.

———

*Episcopal Register, No.* 1, *p* 48.—1315, *December* 22.

Item xi Kalend. Januarii anno quo supra (1315) apud Eccleshale Frater Henricus de Derham monachus de Halys virtute privilegiorum que Abbas et Conventus ejusdem loci obtinent in hac parte, admissus fuit ad vicariam de Walshal ad presentacionem virorum religiosorum verorum ejusdem vicarie patronorum, et institutus in eadem. Et vacavit eadem vicaria per resignacionem Fratris Thome Campion ultimi vicarii ejusdem factam in manibus Domini et ante inquisicionem super hujusmodi vacacionem captam, et mandabatur Archidiacono Staffordie vel ejus officiali quod induceret eum in corporalem possessionem ejusdem sub eadem data.

———

*Episcopal Register, No.* 1, *p.* 89.—1316, *November* 27.

Item v<sup>to.</sup> Kalend. Decembris (1316) apud Aston Frater Thomas Cano-nicus de Hales Oweyn admissus fuit ad vicariam de Walshal vacantem, ad presentacionem Abbatis et Conventus de Hales Oweyn verorum ejusdem vicarie patronorum et institutus canonice in eadem. Et mandabatur, Archidiacono Staffordie vel ejus officiali quod induceret eum in corporalem possessionem ejusdem vicarie. Sub data, &c.

———

*Episcopal Register, No.* 2, *p.* 84.—1348-9, *February* 1.

Item Kalend. Februarii anno Domini supradicto (1348) apud Heywod Frater Nicholaus de Drayton Canonicus Domus de Hales Oweyn, Wyg-orniensis Diocesis, admissus fuit ad vicariam de Walsale vacantem, et institutus in eadem ad presentacionem Abbatis et Conventus de Hales Oweyn predicto verorum ipsius vicarie Patronorum. Et vacavit dicta vicaria per resignacionem Domini Bartholomei de Babynton ultimi vicarii ejusdem. Et mandabatur officiali Archidiaconi de inducendo. Et idem admissus jurans obedienciam.

*Episcopal Register, No. 2, p 151ᵇ—1332, September 14.*

Item xviii Kalend. Octobris anno Domini supradicto (1332) Frater Thomas de Northlech Presbiter monachus Domus de Hales ordinis Premonstratensis admissus fuit ad vicariam de Walsale et institutus in eadem ad presentacionem religiosorum virorum Abbatis et Conventus dicte Domus verorum ejusdem vicarie patronorum. Et vacavit dicta vicaria die Dominica proxime ante Festum Sancti Bartholomei per resignacionem Fratris Thome Campion ultimi vicarii ejusdem. Et manda batur officiali Archidiaconi de inducendo. Et idem admissus jurans obedientiam.

*Episcopal Register, No. 2, p. 169.—1341-2, March 18.*

Item xv Kalend. Aprilis, anno Domini supradicto (1341) apud Heywod, Frater Bartholomeus de Bobyton Canonicus de Hales Oweyn presbiter admissus fuit ad vicariam de Walsale vacantem, et institutus in eadem ad presentacionem Abbatis et Conventus Monasterii de Hales predicto verorum ejusdem vicarie patronorum. Et incepit dicta vicaria vacare iii Nonas Marcii ultimo preteritas, per mortem Fratris Thome Bech ultimi vicarii ejusdem. Et mandabatur officiali Archidiaconi de inducendo. Et idem admissus jurans, &c.

*Episcopal Register, No. 2, p. 181.—1348-9, February 1.*

Item Kalendis Februarii anno Domini supradicto (1348) apud Heywod Frater Nicholaus de Drayton Canonicus domus de Hales Oweyn Wigorniensis Diocesis admissus fuit ad vicariam de Walsale vacantem, et institutus in eadem ad presentacionem Abbatis et Conventus de Hales Oweyn predicto verorum ipsius vicarie patronorum. Et vacavit dicta vicaria per resignacionem domini Bartholomei de Bobynton ultimi vicarii ejusdem. Et mandabatur officiali Archidiaconi de inducendo. Et idem admissus jurans obedienciam.

*Episcopal Register No.* 1, *p.* 18<sup>b</sup>.—1301, *June* 1 *or* 2.

· Item v nonas Junii apud Kenilleworth eodem anno (1301) institutus fuit Thomas de Hales Clericus in ecclesia de Wednesbure ad presentacionem Abbatis et Conventus de Hales.

---

*Episcopal Register*, No, 4, *p.* 50.—1360, *December* 20.

Item xiii Kalend. Januarii anno ut supra (1360) apud Lichfeldiam Frater Willielmus Brommesgrove monachus Monasterii de Hales Oweyu admissus fuit ad vicariam Ecclesie Parochialis de Walsale ad presentacionem religi- osorum virorum Abbatis et Conventus Monasterii predicti verorum ejusdem vicarie patronorum, et institutus in eadem; et vacavit dicta vicaria die Veneris proximo post Festum Saucte Lucie Virginis ultimum preteritum per mortem Fratris Nicholai de Draytton ultimi vicarii ejusdem. Et man dabatur officiario Archidiaconi de inducendo; et ipse juratus juravit obedienciam.

---

*Episcopal Register*, No. 3, *p.* 57<sup>b</sup>.—1366, *April* 4.

Item iiij<sup>to</sup> die Aprilis apud Heywode anno Domini supradicto (1366) Willielmus Bate Presbiter admissus fuit ad Cantariam at altare Sancti Johannis Baptiste in ecclesia de Walsale nuper fundatam, vacantem, ad presentacionem Willielmi Collesone de Walsale veri ejusdem Cantarie patroni et fundatoris; Et institutus in eadem; Et mandabatur officiario Archidiaconi de inducendo.

---

1366, *April* 28.

Item iv Kalend. Maii apud Ichyngton Episcopi anno Domini supradicto (1366) Frater Ricardus de Bruge Canonicus Monasterii de Hales Oweyne admissus fuit ad vicariam ecclesie parochialis de Walsale vacantem. Et institutus in eadem, ad presentacionem Abbatis et Conventus Monasterii predicti verorum ejusdem vicarie patronorum. Et vacavit per creacionem Fratris Willielmi de Brumsgreve ultimi vicarii ejusdem in Abbatem dicti Monasterii. Et idem institutus juravit obedienciam et continuam resi- denciam. Et mandabatur officiario Archidiaconi de inducendo.

---

*Episcopal Register*, No 3, *p.* 66<sup>b</sup>.—1371, *July* 17.

Item xvi Kalend. Augusti apud Heywod anno Domini supradicto (1371) Frater Willielmus de Stoke Canonicus Monasterii de Hales Oweyn Presbiter admissus fuit ad vicariam ecclesie de Walsale vacantem. Et institutus in eadem ad presentacionem Abbatis et Conventus dicti Monasterii verorum ejusdem vicarie patronorum. Et vacavit circa festum Translacionis Sancti Thome eo quod Abbas dicti Monasterii Fratrem Ricardum ultimum dicte vicarie vicarium ad claustrum suum pro certa disciplina monastica recipienda pro certis commissis per eum propeccatis revocavit prout sibi indultum erat.

*Episcopal Register, No. 3, p. 69*<sup>b</sup>.—1375, *July* 23.

Item x Kalend. Augusti, loco et anno Domini supradictis (apud Heywod A.D. 1375) Frater Adam Vaus, Canonicus de Hales Oweyn admissus fuit ad vicariam de Waleshale vacantem, et institutus in eadem ad presentacionem Abbatis et Conventus de Hales Oweyn verorum ejusdem vicarie patronorum. Et vacavit per mortem Fratris Willielmi de Stoke ultimi vicarii ejusdem defuncti. Et idem institutus juravit obedienciam et continuam residenciam. Et mandabatur, &c., ut supra.

*Episcopal Register, No. 3, p. 70*<sup>b</sup>.—1376, *May* 24.

Item ix Kalend. Junii anno Domini et loco supradictis (1376 apud Heywod) Frater Willielmus de Bermyncham presbiter, Canonicus domus de Hales Oweyn admissus fuit ad vicariam ecclesie de Walsale vacantem. Et institutus in eadem ad presentacionem Abbatis et Conventus dicti Monasterii verorum, &c. Et vacavit per mortem Fratris A. de Vaus ultimi vicarii ejusdem. Et mandabatur, &c. Et idem institutus juravit obedienciam et continuam residenciam.

*Episcopal Register, No. 3, p. 73*<sup>b</sup>.—1380, *August* 27.

Item vi Kalend. Septembris anno Domini supradicto (1380) apud Heywode Ricardus de Bloxwych presbiter admissus fuit ad Cantariam Sancti Johannis Baptiste in ecclesia de Walsale vacantem. Et institutus in eadem ad presentacionem Willielmi Coleson de Walshale veri ejusdem cantarie patroni et fundatoris. Et vacavit per mortem Domini Williemi ultimi capellani ejusdem. Et mandabatur officiario de inducendo.

*Episcopal Register, No. 7, p. 74.*—1413, *October* 11.

Item apud Heywode undecimo die mensis Octobris anno Domini prenominato (1413) Frater Henricus de Kyderminster Canonicus Regularis de Hales Oweyn ordinis Premonstratensis Wigornie dioceseos per uendem venerabilem patrem (*i.e.* Dominum Johannem Coven. et Lich. Episcopum) admissus fuit ad vicariam ecclesie parochialis de Walsale dicti patris dioceseos per mortem Fratris Willielmi de Bermyncham ultimi vicarii ejusdem vacantem. Et institutus canonice in eadem cum onere continue et personalis residencie in eadem faciende juxta formam constitucionum legatorum in hoc casu editarum ad presentacionem religiosorum virorum Abbatis et Conventus de Hales Oweyn predicto verorum dicte vicarie patronorum et tandem mandatum fuit Archidiacono seu ejus officiario ad inducendum ipsum, etc.

*Episcopal Register, No. 9, p. 48ᵇ·—1422, December 28.*

Item apud Eccleshale xxviii die mensis Decembris anno Domini supradicto (1422) per Dominum admissus fuit Frater Thomas Walsale Canonicus Monasterii de Halys Oweyn presbiter ad vicariam ecclesie parochialis de Walsale dicti patris dioceseos vacantem, et vicarius perpetuus canonice institutus in eadem cum suis juribus et pertinenciis universis ad presentacionem religiosorum virorum Abbatis et Conventus de Halys Oweyn predicto verorum ipsius vicarie patronorum. Et idem institutus jurans continuam residenciam ut in forma constitutus et obedienciam. Et obtinuit litteras Archidiacono seu ejus officiario directas ad inducendum eundem. Et vacare incepit dicta vicaria die mensis Decembris per creacionem Fratris Henrici ultimi vicarii ibidem in Abbatem prefati Monasterii de Halys Oweyn.

*Episcopal Register, No. 9, p. 59ᵇ·—1430-1, February 26.*

Item xxvi mensis Februarii anno Domini supradicto (1430) Frater Ricardus Worfelde Canonicus Regularis Monasterii de Hales Oweyn admissus fuit ad perpetuam vicariam ecclesie parochialis de Walshale per liberam resignationem Fratris Thome de Walshale ultimi vicarii ad presentacionem Abbatis et Conventus Monasterii de Hales Oweyn.

*Episcopal Register, No. 10, p. 14ᵇ·—1447, November 23.*

Item apud Lichfield xxiii die mensis Novembris anno Domini memorato (1447)—admissus fuit Dominus Ricardus Marchald presbiter ad perpetuam

H

Cantariam ad altare Sancti Johannis Baptiste in ecclesia parochiali de Walsale fundatam, per mortem Domini Rogeri Spuryour ultimi capellani ejusdem vacantem—ad presentacionem nobilis mulieris Domine Johanne relicte Henrici Beaumont militis et Ricardi Whithill domicelli verorum ipsius Cantarie patronorum.

*Episcopal Register, No.* 10, *p.* 15.—1448, *May* 8.

A.D. 1448. Item apud Beaudesert octavo decimo die mensis Maij anno Domini predicto—admissus fuit ad ecclesiam parochialem de Wednesbury Dominus Johannis Brounfield presbiter ac Rector institutus canonice in eadem—ad donacionem Excellentissimi in Christo principis et Domini nostri Henrici Dei gracia Regis Anglie et Ffrancie et Domini Hibernie illustris veri ipsius ecclesie patroni, etc.

*Episcopal Register, No.* 11, *p.* 17ᵇ.—1458-9, *January* 25.

Item xxv die mensis Januarij anno Domini 1458 apud Beaudesert ad missus fuit Frater Thomas Nechelis Canonicus Monasterii Beate Marie de Hales Owen ad vicariam perpetuam ecclesie parochialis de Walshale per mortem Fratris Ricardi Worfelde ultimi vicarii ibidem vacantem—ad presentacionem religiosorum virorum Abbatis et Conventus de Hales Owen ipsius vicarie verorum patronorum.

*Episcopal Register, No* 12, *p.* 42.—1462-3, *February* 4.

1462-3, February 4. Frater Johannes Comber Canonicus Regularis Monasterii Beate Marie Virginis de Hales Owen admissus fuit ad vicariam perpetuam ecclesie parochialis de Walsale per liberam resignacionem Fratris Thome Nechelis ultimi vicarii ejusdem vacantem—ad presentacionem Abbatis, etc.

*Episcopal Register, No.* 12, *p.* 53 —1485, *March* 30.

1485. Penultimo die Marcii—admissus fuit Dominus Rogerus Wryght ad Cantariam perpetuam ad altare S. Johannis Baptiste in ecclesia parochiali de Walshehall per liberam resignationem Magˢ⁺ Thome Warde ultimi cappellani ibidem vacantem—ad presentacionem Georgii Stanley et Domine Elianore uxoris ejusdem et Henrici Vernon Armigeri ipsius Cantarie hac vice patronorum. Et mandabatur, &c.

*Episcopal Register, No. 12, p. 60ᵇ.—1489, December 15.*

1489, 15 December. Johannes Seed Canonicus de Hales Owen admissus ad perpetuam vicariam de Walshall per liberam resignacionem Fratris Henrici Eggebaston ultimi vicarii ad presᵐ· Abbatis et Conventus, etc.

---

*Episcopal Register, No. 13, p. 143ᵇ.—1493, May 8.*

1493, May 8. Admissus fuit Dominus Robertus Doore ad Cantariam perpetuam in ecclesia parochiali de Walsall ad altare Sancti Johannis Baptiste—per mortem Rogeri Wryght ultimi capellarii ejusdem vacantem —ad presentacionem Domini Henrici Vernon militis et Johannis Beaumont Armigeri verorum dicte Cantarie patronorum.

---

*Episcopal Register, No. 13, p. 210.—1499, May 11.*

1499, May 11. Admissus fuit Dominus Willielmus Taylor ad ecclesiam parochialem de Walsall per mortem naturalem ffratris Johannis Sedde ultimi vicarii ejusdem vacantem ad presentacionem Abbatis, etc. de Hales Owen.

---

*Episcopal Register, No. 14, p. 45ᵇ.—1543-4, February 3.*

1543-4, February 3. Admissus Thomas Dobson capellanus ad Cantariam perpetuam Sancti Johannis Baptiste in ecclesia parochiali de Walsall fundatam, per mortem magistri Roberti Dore vacantem—ad presentacionem Johannis Vicecomitis Lisle Baronis de Malpasse et Somerey Domini Bassett et Tyas nobilisque ordinis Garterii militis necnon magni admiralli Anglie et Hibernie veri dicte cantarie hac vice patroni eo quod Georgius Vernon et Humfridus Cumberford armigeri indubitati dicte Cantarie patroni capellanum suum infra mensem integrum a tempore vacacionis ejusdem Cantarie ad ipsam non presentaverunt, etc.

---

*Episcopal Register, No. 14, p. 47ᵇ.—1546-7, February 1.*

1546-7, February 1. Admissus fuit Dominus Thomas Burne ad Cantariam perpetuam fundatam per Thomam Moseley generosum in ecclesia parochiali de Walsall, per mortem Domini Henrici Hynks ultimi possess-oris ejusdem vacantem—ad presentacionem Edwardi Lyttelton de Pillet-nall in com. Staff. armigeri veri et indubitati dicte Cantarie patroni.

---

*Episcopal Register, No. 14, p. 47^b.—1547, April 19.*

1547, xix die Aprilis. Admissus Thomas Baynes capellanus ad vicariam perpetuam ecclesie parochialis de Wednesburye—per mortem naturalem Domini Ricardi Genyns ultimi vicarii ejusdem vacantem—ad presenta-cionem Johannis Comitis Warwic Domini magni Camerarii Anglie veri et indubitati dicte vicarie patroni.

---

*Episcopal Register, No. 14, p. 48.—1548, October 6.*

1548, vi die Octobris. Admissus Willielmus Starismore clericus ad vicariam perpetuam de Wednesbury—per mortem Thome Banes ultimi vicarii vacantem—ad presentacionem Johannis Comitis Warwic, etc.

---

*Episcopal Register, No. 15, p. 64.—1569, November 11.*

1569, November 11. Admissus Robertus Weston ad vicariam per-petuam ecclesie parochialis de Wallsall per mortem Johannis Turner ultimi incumbentis—ad presentacionem Georgii Clarkson hac vice patroni racione cujusdam dimissionis Rectorie de Wallsall pro termino annorum, etc.

---

*Episcopal Register, No. 15, p. 74.—1574-5, March 12.*

1574, xii Marcii. Admissus Robertus Willson ad vicariam ecclesie de Walsall, per resignacionem Rob. Weston vacantem—ad presentacionem Georgii Clerkson hac vice patroni.

---

*Episcopal Register, No. 16, p. 2.—1619, April 7.*

1619, April 7. Richard Dolphin, B.A., instituted Vicar of Wednes-bury, on death of last incumbent, on presentation of King James.

*Terrier of* 1612.—*Wednesbury, October 4th, A.D.* 1612.

*The Terrier of the Glebe Land and other Tythe belonging to the Vicarage there.*

1mprimis.   One cottage with a cartilage and garden adjoining to it, containing by estimation half an acre of ground or thereabouts, and also one barn, together, situate, lying, and being between the King's highway there, leading from Walsall toward the town of Wednesbury and Churchgate Bridge, and by one other highway leading from Walsall aforesaid towards the church of Wednesbury, the land of Richard Watson, in the tenure of William Babbe, and a common field there, called the Gill Church Field, on all part.

Item.   Tithe hay in kind.   Wool and lamb, and also tithe of all other titheable thing within the parish of Wednesbury.   The tithe of corn only excepted and foreprized.

Item.   The Easter Book, viz., of every householder, fivepence ; of servant that takes wages, fourpence ; of every other labourer, fourpence ; and of every other communicant, twopence.

Item.   Mortuaries and churchwailes of weddings, christenings, and burials there.

Item.   Five shillings and eightpence grave money for every one that is buried in the high chancel of the same church.

Per me, RICHARD DOLPHINE, cler. vicar, ibm.

RICHARD BROWN, × his mark,
GEORGE HOULDIN, ×     } Churchwardens.

---

*Terrier of* 1726.—*July 8th,* 1726.

*A true and perfect Terrier, shewing all lands, houses, tithes, and other profits, belonging to the vicarage of Wednesbury.*

Imprⁱˢ. The Vicarage House, consisting of 4 bays of building, being 2 stories high, with a little study and a closet over it, the same at the west end thereof, with one shiard and washouse adjoining to the said house, and also one bay of building, called the brewhouse, adjoining to the aforesaid house.

One barn and stable, consisting of 2 bays of building, adjoining to the said brewhouse, with a pigstye adjoining to the said stable, all which are in good repair, and are butted and bounded on the north side by the lane that leads from the church tow<sup>ds.</sup> Wood Green, and on the south side to the vicarige garden and fold-yard, butted on the east to the lane which leads from a place call'd Oaks Well to Wood Green, and on the west to a certain garden, in the occupation of Tho<sup>s.</sup> Browne, with a small fold-yard and garden, consisting of about a quar. of an acre of ground, butting on the east to the lane which leads from Oaks Well to Wood Green, and on the west to the garden of the afores<sup>d.</sup> Tho<sup>s.</sup> Browne ; and on the north, bounded to the said house and barn ; and on the south, by a certain garden of Joseph Freemans, of Walsall, and now in the occupation of Tho. Hall, of Wednesbury.  A large churchyard, with a stone wall round about it.

### EASTER ROLLS.

|  | s. | d. |
|---|---|---|
| A married couple | 0 | 6 |
| A young single person | 0 | 4 |
| An apprentice, aged 16 years | 0 | 4 |
| A milking cow | 0 | 1 |
| A barren cow | 0 | 1½ |
| An year old heifer | 0 | 1 |

### TYTHE EGGS.

For an hen two, and a cock three.

For a duck two, and a drake three.

Pro Horto and Fumo, 2<sup>d.</sup> which the minister gives to the clarke for attendance of him.

### TYTHE OF SHEEP AND LAMBS.

For every individual sheep, 1<sup>d.</sup> and for every individual lamb, 3<sup>d.</sup>  For summering or wintering of sheep, if sold or taken out of the parish, for every score for each month, 4<sup>d.</sup> payable to the vicar; for all fforeigners lambs which are fallen in his parish, for each lamb, 3<sup>d.</sup>; and if their sheep are sheard in the parish, 1<sup>d.</sup> and a lamb, ½.  Calves—if seven, one is due to the vicar, without any deduction to the owner; if under seven, nothing payable to the vicar ; if fourteen, two, without deduction.

For each colt foled in the parish, payable to the vicar, 1<sup>s.</sup> 0<sup>d.</sup> ; and for each pack horse, annually, 1<sup>s.</sup> 0<sup>d.</sup>

## TYTHE PIGGS.

If seven, one to the vicar, without deduction.

If two sows happen to farry near the same time together and have fourteen pigs, the vicar takes two, without deduction, and if twenty no more.

## TYTHE GEESE.

If seven, one to the vicar; if fourteen, two, without deduction, and if twenty no more.

Fish, if sold out of the ponds, the 10th value thereof is payable to the vicar.

Honey, payable to the vicar, the 10th pound.

Apples and peares, due to the vicar, the 10th peck and half peck.

## TYTHE OF HEMP AND FFLAX.

For every peck of hemp sowed in garden or backside, 0ˢ. 6ᵈ.

For every peck of flax sowed in garden or backside, 0ˢ. 7¼ᵈ.

For flax or hemp sowed in the fields or inclosures, payable in kind; tythe of plants, if sold, yᵉ 10th thereof payable to the vicar.

Turnips and carrots, the 10th thereof payable to the vicar.

Herbage of forreigners, 2ˢ in yᵉ pound, if required by the minister.

## SURPLICE FEES.

|  | £ | s. | d. |
|---|---|---|---|
| For churching of a woman . . . | 0 | 0 | 8 |
| For the publication of the banns is freely given to the vicar . . . . | 0 | 2 | 6 |
| For marrying by banns . . . | 0 | 2 | 6 |
| For marraige by licence . . . | 0 | 5 | 0 |
| For the burial of a person in the church . | 0 | 1 | 0 |
| For a burial in the communion chancel . | 0 | 1 | 0 |
| And for breaking up the ground in the said chancel . . . . . | 0 | 10 | 0 |
| Paid to the vicar (Mr. Ward's and Mr. Hoo's families being exempted) for preaching a funeral sermon . . . . | 0 | 10 | 0 |
| If a text be chose for the minister . . | 1 | 0 | 0 |
| For a burial in the churchyard . . | 0 | 0 | 8 |
| For breaking open the ground for a still-born child . . . . . | 0 | 0 | 4 |

## MORTUARIES.

If the goods of the deceased are worth ten marks, 3ˢ· 4ᵈ· is payable to the vicar.

If the goods of the deceased are worth £30, to the vicar, 6ˢ· 8ᵈ·; if worth £40, payable to the vicar, 10ˢ· 0ᵈ·

## TYTHE HAY.

The tythe thereof payable to the vicar in kind, excepting one meadow, belonging to Mr. Thoˢ· Addes, of Barr Maggney, lyeing at the Delves, and adjoining to Barr parish, which meadow pays to the vicar 1ˢ· pʳ annum.

There is no other modus for hay belonging to any of the parishioners or any other person.   One close of land lately divided into two, lyeing at Shelfield Butts, in the parish of Walsall, belonging to the vicar and poor of Wednesbury, containing four or five acres, lately in the possession of John Row, and now let of a lease by Edwᵈ· Best, late vicar, and Willᵐ· Nickin and Henry Wood, late churchwardens, to William House, of Shelfield Butts, for the space of 21 years, the lease being kept in the chest of the parish church of Wednesbury.   The rent thereof is £2 pʳ annum, £1 whereof is payable to the vicar on the feast of S. Michael the Archangel, annually, for preaching four lecture sermons on four festival or fast days, the other £1 to be paid to the churchwardens for the use of the poor, on Good Friday, for ever.

## CLERK'S WAGES

Are £3 per annum, paid to him by the churchwardens—£1 10ˢ· upon the Festival of S. John the Baptist, and the other £1 10ˢ· upon the Festival of S. Thomas; and for a grave in the churchyard, payable to the clerk, 1ˢ·; and for ringing the passing bell, 1ˢ·; and for ringing after the funeral, 1ˢ· each hour.

EDWARD EGINTON, Vicar.

JOSEPH COLLINS,   }
SIMEON ROBINSON, } Churchwardens.

In a terrier taken in 1730, it states that—

There is a very great coal mine in the parish, which is prejudicial to the vicar, by destroying a great deal of ground otherways profitable to him.

The most learned in the law allow that if tithe is not due (which is a query), yet satisfaction ought to be made for the land rendered useless. Mr. Sergeant Hoo was of that opinion, who was Lord of the Manor and master of a considerable part of the mine, and yearly during his life gave two guineas towards damages, as likewise did the Honourable Mr. Ward, another of the proprietors, and Mr. Sparrow the same, as he rented the mines ; but now it is wholly fallen into the hands of Quakers.

I

# CHAPTER IV.

## Benefactions.

---

We have now the pleasure to transcribe the names and benefactions of those charitable persons who bequeathed example and evidence to the *present* and *future* generations of Wednesbury, " that as the tree is known by its fruit, so living faith will be manifested in good works, which God hath ordained that we should walk in them."

Sir Henry Beaumont, Knt., Lord of the Manor of Wednesbury, by will, dated Nov. 10th, 1471, directed that his body should be buried in the parish church of Wednesbury, and left for the use of the said church one hundred shillings.

John Comberford, Gentleman, of the parish of Wednesbury, by his will, dated April 23rd, 1559, gave to the churchwardens six and eightpence "to bestow on the church;" also, another "six and eightpence to the church for his burial." He also directed that his body should be buried in the parish church of Wednesbury.

Thomas Parkes, Gentleman, gave by will, dated January 11th, 1602, to the poor people of Wednesbury ten pounds, to be paid yearly by twenty shillings a year to the vicar of Wednesbury and the churchwardens, to the use of the poor, to be given every Good Friday, for ten years." Also the said Thomas Parkes gave a school-house, a certain tenement in Wednesbury, and a close, called " Clay Pit Leasowe," to maintain a schoolmaster to teach ten poor children of the parish, for the term of fourscore years after his decease. He also gave a cottage, situate in Wednesbury, to be set apart as an almshouse, for two persons, for ever.*

Richard Parkes, Esquire, son of the above Thomas, did by will confirm the above, and gave forty shillings more to the school, A.D. 1617.

Dorothy Parkes, wife of the said Richard, gave a silver cup, with a cover, to be a communion cup for the church. It has the following inscription :—" The gift of Mrs. Dorothy Parkes, wife of Richard Parkes, Esq., deceased. Given A.D. 1629." Also she gave 20 shillings yearly for four sermons to be preached in this church on *four festival days*, yearly, for ever ; and 20 shillings to the poor, yearly, for ever, to be paid from a close, called the Butts, lying in Shelfield. This close of land produced £7 per annum in 1808 ; one-half was paid to the vicar, and the other half to the poor.

Walter Stanley, of West Bromwich, Esq., by will, dated February 11th, 1613, gave to the poor of the parish of Wednesbury three pounds.

William Comberford, Esq., Lord of the Manor, gave the use of £20, by will, to be bestowed, for ever, every Good Friday, on the poor, in bread, A.D. 1626.

John Shelton, of West Bromwich, Esq , by will, dated February 8th, 1664, gave to the poor of Wednesbury ten pounds of lawful money.

Richard Jennings, yeoman, gave 30 shillings, yearly, for ever, to the poor of this parish—20 of it to be distributed on New Year's Day, and the other 10 shillings on Good Friday. Twenty shillings to be paid by Mr. Francis Tomkiss and his heirs for ever, for the close called King's Hill, adjoining to King's Hill Field, and for land in Monway Field ; and for one croft of land lying between Heathfields and the way leading between Monway Gate and Wednesbury Bridge ; and the other 10 shillings to be paid by Richard Hopkins and his heirs for ever.

Edward Dudley, of Tipton, left by will, in the year 1652, the sum of £100, the interest thereof to be paid, yearly, to the use of the poor of four parishes, viz., 40s. to the poor of Tipton, 20s. to the poor of Sedgley, 20s.

* This almshouse is lost. It would, perhaps, be as well if some of the inhabitants of Wednesbury were to endeavour to find out what is become of this and other " charities" not now enjoyed by the parish.

to the poor of Bilston, and 20s. to the poor of Wednesbury; to be distributed in two equal parts, the one at Midsummer Day, and the other at S. Thomas's Day, by the churchwardens and overseers.

Joseph Hopkins, of Birmingham, died 31st of January, 1683, and by will, dated April 7th, 1681, gave £200 to be laid out in land for the use of the poor of this parish. Land was accordingly purchased at or near Moxley, in the parish of Darlaston, adjoining this parish, known by the names of Hoo Marsh, and Cranberry or Cranbarrow Hills, containing by estimation sixteen acres, or thereabouts, and the same remains invested in trustees. The mines under this land have been sold by the trustees, who have invested the money, viz., £1,800, in the Three per Cent. Conso. lidated Annuities, in the names of the Reverend Isaac Clarkson, John Addison, and Simeon Constable, being part of the said trustees of this charity. The Three per Cent. Consols produce £54 per annum; to which must be added the yearly rent of the land. Part of this income is disposed of annually in coats and gowns upon S. Thomas's Day, and the residue in bread and money, on the Friday before Whit Sunday, to such of the poor inhabitants of this parish as have not received parochial relief for twelve months previously.

Elizabeth Beck, of this town, ordered by will, in the year 1702, the payment of ten shillings annually out of three houses in this town, to the use of the poor born in the parish of Wednesbury, two of which houses she left to Joseph Nightingale and Samuel Hide, her two executors, and the other house to Isabel Holden and her heirs and executors, she or they paying the aforesaid executors and their heirs two shillings yearly, to be given on S. Thomas's Day, by the churchwardens and overseers.

John Heaton, of Wednesbury, by will, in the year 1753, directed ten shillings a year to be paid to the churchwardens of this parish, on the 24th of December, to be disposed of by them to twenty of the poorest persons, men or women, in this parish—sixpence each, and charged on a house and premises in Bridge-street, in this town. This property came into the hands of Jonathan Perkins.

William Holden, of Birmingham, merchant, by will, left forty shillings annually to be given to the poor of this parish,—payable from the Three per Cent. Consols, the vicar and churchwardens being trustees for the same.

Ambrose Tibbetts, of Church Aston, in the county of Salop, in the year 1815, bequeathed £100 to be invested, and directed the minister and churchwardens, and overseers of the poor of this parish, to divide the interest in equal shares to ten poor decayed tradesmen or housekeepers of the age of fifty years or upwards, resident in this parish, not receiving alms or parochial relief, on the feast day of S. Thomas, yearly for ever. The legacy duty of £10 was deducted, and the remainder was invested in the New Four per Cent. Annuities, in the names of the Rev. Alexander Bunn Haden, Isaiah Danks, William Lees, and Josiah Stone.

Thomas Watkins, of Ardwick, near Manchester, in the year 1826, bequeathed £600 to be invested; and directed the vicar and churchwardens of this parish to apply the interest of £400 in providing for six poor men and six poor women, belonging to this parish, who shall regularly attend divine service in the parish church—one coat, with suitable linen, to each poor man, and one gown, with suitable linen, to each poor woman—on Christmas Day, yearly, or ever. The interest of £200 in providing for twelve poor women, qualified as abovementioned—one loaf each of good wheaten bread, on the first Sunday in every month. The widow of the testator generously paid the legacy duty (£60), which otherwise must have been deducted. The above £600 was invested in the New Four per Cent. Annuities, in the names of Stephen Faulkner Crowther, Samuel Addison, and John Addison.

Stephen Faulkner Crowther, of Wednesbury, solicitor, by will, dated November 23rd, 1829, bequeathed to the minister and churchwardens of the parish of Wednesbury for the time being £300, upon trust, to invest the same, and to divide the yearly interest thereof, according to their discretion, amongst poor persons regularly attending Divine service in the parish church. The sum of £306 10s. Stock, New Three-and-a-Half per Cent. was purchased September 14, 1830, in the names of the Rev. Isaac Clarkson, vicar, and John Addison and John Russell, churchwardens.

Thomas Rowlinson, of this parish, in the year 1821, bequeathed £100 to be invested—and directed the churchwardens to expend the interest in the purchase of bread—to be distributed amongst such poor persons, inhabitants of this parish, as they shall think proper, on Good Friday, yearly, for ever. The legacy duty (£10) was given by George Watkin Court. The above was invested in the New Four per Cent. Annuities, in the names of John Addison and John Parkes.

Thomas Griffiths, late of West Bromwich, by will, dated the 4th of May, 1848, gave the sum of £100 (duty free) to the vicar and churchwardens for the time being of the parish church of Wednesbury, to be by them invested at interest on real security; the income thereof is to be received by them, and laid out each year for ever in the purchase of 100 loaves of bread, and on the last day of July annually to distribute the same among 100 poor widows resident in the parish of Wednesbury.

Samuel Addison, late of this town, banker, by will, dated April 22nd, 1849, gave the sum of £2000, duty free. The annual income arising therefrom is for ever to be laid out and applied by the vicar and churchwardens of the parish church of Wednesbury for the time being, in the purchase and finding of such suitable coats, gowns, and other articles of dress or bedding, as they or a majority of them shall think fit; and on the feast day of S. Thomas in each year for ever shall give and distribute the same unto such poor men and poor women (inhabitants of the parish of Wednesbury) as they or a major part of them shall deem fit and proper objects of this charity. The sum thus given is invested by his trustees (the Rev. I. Clarkson, Philip Williams, and Addison Russell) in the purchase of £2141 18s. in the Three per Cent. Consols. He also gave the sum of £1000, duty free; the annual income arising thereof is for ever to be applied by the incumbent and churchwardens of the new parish of S. John, Wednesbury, on Christmas Day and five other days in each year, to the purchasing of bread and other necessaries for such poor men and poor women of the parish of S. John, as the minister and churchwardens shall think proper. The amount thus given is invested in the names of his trustees, in the purchase of £1070 19s. 3d. in the Three per Cent. Consols.

F OFFLOW SOUT H.

*dens of the several Parishes and Town-*
*th June, 1816.*

*ommons in 1787, after the Abstract of*

| al be of ey. | Clear Annual Produce of that given in Land after deducting the Rents issuing thereout. | OBSERVATIONS. | |
|---|---|---|---|
| . | . . . . | Never enjoyed by the Poor. | |
| 0 | . . . . | Was son of the above testator, and confirmed the donation by will, also with the addition of said 40s. per annum to a schoolmaster, but we cannot learn that these gifts were ever claimed or taken into possession. | |
| . | 1 0 0 | | |
| . | . . . . | Never received. Circular is 30s. regularly paid. | |
| . | . . . . | | |
| 0 | . . . . | | |
| 0 | . . . . | | |
| . . | 0 10 0 | | |
| . . | 1 0 0 | | |
| . . | 0 10 0 | | |
| . . | 1 0 0 | | |

.

# Churchwardens and Overseers.

---

| CHURCHWARDENS. | OVERSEERS. |
|---|---|

1561 to 1598  Nicholas Tonkes,
           Thomas Meryhurst.

1599  Thomas Hopkins,
     Edward Syddon.

1600  Thomas Dolphine,
     John Hawke.

1601-2-3  John Poynder,
        John Mathen.

1604-5-6  Samuel Addenbrooke,
        William Babbe.

1607-8-9  Henry Sheldon,
        Thomas Hurbbutt.

1610  Francis Tonkys,
     William Hebbeard.

1611  Thomas Tonks,
     George Medewe.

1612-13  George Holdin,
       Richd. Browne, his ⋈ mark

1614-15  Thomas Cowy,
       Thomas Parkshouse,

1616-17  Francis Pool,
       Henry Pool.

1618  William Hopkins,
     George Bassett.

1619  John Becke,
     Richard Sheldon.

1620  Henry Hurbbut,
     Richard Wilkes.

CHURCHWARDENS.                    OVERSEERS.

1621  Thomas Biram,
      George Siddowne.
1622  Henry Siddowne,
      Richard Salte.
1623  William Hopkins,
      Nicholas Field.
1624  John Willis,
      Robert Nightingale.
1625  George Darlaston,
      Henry Morris.
1626  Henry Nightingale,
      John Browne
1627  Richard Hart.
      [Name not legible in the Register.]
1628  William Hopkins.
      Edward Watson.
1629-30  Francis Perry,
           Richard Jarratt.
1631  Henry Addenbrooke,
      Humphrey Tonkys.
1632  John Carter,
      Richard Sylvester.
1633  Simon Warde,
      William Terry.
1634  William Hopkins,
      Thomas Cowy.
1635  Thomas Jefferson,
      William Hawkes.
1636  Henry Siddowne,
      John Hampson the younger.
1637  Richard Sheldon,
      Henry Siddowne.


There is no record of churchwardens in the Parish
Register during the Commonwealth.

| | CHURCHWARDENS. | OVERSEERS. |
|---|---|---|
| 1676 | Thomas Hide, Thomas Hawkes. | |
| 1677 | Henry Aston, John Chester. | |
| 1678 | Joseph Tibbutts, Samuel Welsh. | |
| 1679 | Thomas Jesson, Henry Bassett. | John Tuncks, William Hopkin. |
| 1680 | Thomas Meadew, Henry Wood. | |
| 1681 | | |
| 1682 | Thomas Hind, Philip Harrison. | |
| 1683 | John Snape, John Chester, jun. | Thomas Jesson, Thomas Hind. |
| 1684 | William Tibbutts, jun. Abram Parks. | |
| 1685 | Richard Right, Richard Dunton. | John Hunks, John Fidoe. |
| 1686 | Josiah Freeman, Edward Whitehouse. | Henry Aston, Richard Hollyhead. |
| 1687 | James Silvester, John Belshar. | William Smallwood, William Constable. |
| 1688 | | |
| 1689 | | |
| 1690 | | Thomas Haines, James Silvester. |
| 1691 | | Thomas Jesson, Richard Budler. |
| 1692 | | |
| 1693 | William Holden, jun. Henry Jackson. | |
| 1694 | | Josiah Freeman. |
| 1695 | Richard Smith, George Silvester. | |

K

| | CHURCHWARDENS. | OVERSEERS. |
|---|---|---|
| 1696 | | |
| 1697 | | |
| 1698 | Richard Edge, Richard Hanson. | |
| 1699 | John Mountford, Henry Wood. | |
| 1700 | Humphrey Kendrick, Thomas Saunders. | |
| 1701 | John Cox, Samuel Hide. | |
| 1702 | Thomas Wright, Richard Darby. | |
| 1703 | Alexander Bunn, Richard Lane. | |
| 1704 | John Belshar, Daniel More. | |
| 1705 | John Belshar, Daniel More. | |
| 1706 | John Russell, John Cashmore. | |
| 1707 | | |
| 1708 | | |
| 1709 | | |
| 1710 | | |
| 1711 | | |
| 1712 | | |
| 1713 | Thomas Brown, Richard Tebbits. | |
| 1714 | Humphrey Kendrick, Thomas Jesson. | |
| 1715 | | |
| 1716 | | |
| 1717 | George Hunt, Samuel Bruerton. | |
| 1718 | | |

# Baptisms, Marriages, and Burials.

| DATE. | BAPTISMS. | MARRIAGES. | BURIALS. |
|---|---|---|---|
| 1561...No register | | | 7 |
| 1562 | | 12 | 14 |
| 1563 | | 6 | 15 |
| 1564 | | 15 | 10 |
| 1565 | | 3 | 11 |
| 1566 | | 1 | 10 |
| 1567 | | 3 | 10 |
| 1568 | | 2 | 8 |
| 1569 | 16 | | 18 |
| 1570 | 30 | 6 | 15 |
| 1571 | 21 | 7 | 22 |
| 1572... 7 (the rest are missing) | | 3 | 18 |
| 1573 | | 10 | 11 |
| 1574 | | 6 | 9 |
| 1575 | | 5 | 13 |
| 1576 | | 2 | 13 |
| 1577 | | 4 | 15 |
| 1578 | | 7 | 11 |
| 1579 | | 9 | 24 |
| 1580 | | All lost but | 2 |
| 1581 | | 3 | |
| 1582...All lost but 5 | | 12 | |
| 1583 | 23 | 5 | |
| 1584 | 39 | 5 | |
| 1585 | 24 | 3 | |
| 1586 | 18 | 3 | |
| 1587 | 31 | 9 | |

| DATE. | BAPTISMS. | MARRIAGES. | BURIALS. |
|---|---|---|---|
| 1588 | 29 | 14 | |
| 1589 | 87 | 16 | |
| 1590 | 86 | 6 | |
| 1591 | 20 | 6 All lost but | 12 |
| 1592 | 88 | 4 | 24 |
| 1593 | 81 | | 15 |
| 1594 | | | 19 |
| 1595 | 27 | | 23 |
| 1596 | 37 | | 31 |
| 1597 | 18 | 9 | 44 |
| 1598 | 25 | 16 | 85 |
| 1599 | 43 | 8 | 28 |
| 1600 | 86 | 5 All lost but | 13 |
| 1601 | 23 | | 9 |
| 1602 | | | 27 |
| 1603 | } 69 | | 12 |
| 1604 | | | 24 |
| 1605 | 29 | | 21 |
| 1606 | 82 | | 41 |
| 1607 | 40 | | 19 |
| 1608 | 28 | | 83 |
| 1609 | 82 | | 10 |
| 1610 | 83 | | 24 |
| 1611 | 88 | | 22 |
| 1612 | 30 | | 21 |
| 1613 | 88 | 5 | 17 |
| 1614...All lost but | 21 | 3 | |
| 1615 | 10 | 6 | 26 |
| 1616 | 28 | 7 | 21 |
| 1617 | 81 | 9 | 15 |
| 1618 | 44 | 10 | 23 |
| 1619 | 83 | | 22 |
| 1620 | 42 | | 80 |
| 1621 | 89 | | 25 |
| 1622 | 30 | | 28 |
| 1623 | 25 | | 86 |

| DATE. | BAPTISMS. | MARRIAGES. | BURIALS. |
|---|---|---|---|
| 1624 | 37 | | 38 |
| 1625 | 38 | | 30 |
| 1626 | 27 | | 19 |
| 1627 | 33 | | 29 |
| 1628 | 36 All lost but | 6 | 17 |
| 1629 | 33 | 8 | 24 |
| 1630 | 32 | 10 All lost but | 2 |
| 1631 | 24 | 8 | |
| 1632 | 30 | 12 | |
| 1633 | 35 | 8 | |
| 1634 | 28 | 10 | |
| 1635 | 38 | 7 | |
| 1636 | 44 | 9 | |
| 1637 | 30 | 6 | |
| 1638 | 30 All lost but | 4 | |
| 1639 | 46 | | |
| 1640 | 38 | | |
| 1641 | 49 | | |
| 1642 | 18 | | |
| 1643 | 3 | | |
| 1644 | 6 | | |
| 1645 | 12 | | |
| 1646 | 4 | | |
| 1647 | | | |
| 1648 to 1663 | No Register. | | |
| 1664 | 9 | | |
| 1665 | 14 | 1 | |
| 1666 | 32 | 13 | 30 |
| 1667 | 53 | 5 | 43 |
| 1668 | 39 | 8 | 14 |
| 1669 | 37 | 7 | 28 |
| 1670 | 55 | 5 | 37 |
| 1671 | 40 | 11 | 20 |
| 1672 | 48 | 14 | 25 |
| 1673 | 58 | 8 | 35 |
| 1674 | 32 | 3 | 34 |

| DATE. | BAPTISMS. | MARRIAGES. | BURIALS. |
|---|---|---|---|
| 1675 | 41 | 14 | 22 |
| 1676 | 52 | 12 | 39 |
| 1677 | 41 | 6 | 37 |
| 1678 | 50 | 18 All lost but | 6 |
| 1679 | 65 | 13 | 37 |
| 1680 | 46 | 4 | 25 |
| 1681 | 46 | 10 | 39 |
| 1682 | 57 | 12 | 22 |
| 1683 | 56 | 7 | 43 |
| 1684 | 58 | 9 | 62 |
| 1685 | 53 | 5 | 52 |
| 1686 | 55 | 9 | 40 |
| 1687 | 59 | 14 | 29 |
| 1688 | 42 | 4 | 57 |
| 1689 | 36 | 14 | 31 |
| 1690 | 51 | 9 | 24 |
| 1691 | 51 | 7 | 24 |
| 1692 | 33 | 2 | 25 |
| 1693 | 32 | 11 | 37 |
| 1694 | 29 | 4 | 10 |
| 1695 | 50 | 9 | 42 |
| 1696 | 46 | 5 | 17 |
| 1697 | 45 | 8 | 44 |
| 1698 | 58 | 5 | 70 |
| 1699 | 20 | 12 | 33 |
| 1700 | 58 | 10 | 41 |
| 1701 | 41 | 10 | 37 |
| 1702 | 60 | 65 | 21 |
| 1703 | 45 | 11 | 28 |

## CHAPTER V.

## The Modern Town.

-------

It will be seen from the preceding pages that Wednesbury is not only a very ancient place, but that it has been subjected to many vicissitudes. The modern town presents a very different appearance to the eye from the town of other days, both as regards its population, its manufactures, its railways and canals, its churches and schools. Those portions which were once forest, or at least well wooded, and which added to the beauty and variety of the scenery around, are now the seats of mining and manufacturing operations; and in consequence of the increasing smoke and sulphureous exhalations arising therefrom, the oaks, which formerly thrived here, together with other trees and herbage, have languished and died. The parish has nearly lost its rural population, and is now become the busy hive of shopkeepers, mechanics, miners, and ironworkers.

The inhabitants have been more or less affected by the changes that have taken place in the religion of the country,—in the manners, customs, and habits which have succeeded each other,—in the administration of the law, and in the government of the kingdom,—from the despotic rule of the Druidical priesthood to the mild sway of Queen Victoria,—from rude barbarism to modern civilisation,—from the serfdom and vassalage of the feudal system to the enjoyment of full liberty under the shadow of our unparalleled constitution,—from the idolatrous worship and bloody rites of Druidism to the worship of the Triune God,—from the corrupt system of the Papacy, and the usurpation of the Bishop of Rome, to the enjoyment of pure and undefiled religion, restored at the glorious period of the Reformation, which, with its attendant blessings, has been preserved and handed down to the present day.

Notwithstanding the great change that has taken place in the appearance of the surrounding country, there are but few places which afford so extensive and striking a panorama of the mine and metal district as Wednesbury Hill, " taking in," as a modern historian expresses it, " within its lofty glance the burning, fiery furnaces of West Bromwich, Tipton, Coseley, Bilston, and Darlaston; the horizon, miles upon miles, dotted about with smoking, blazing coke hearths, appears under the black, sooty roof of nightfall, like a large illuminated minster, devoted to a ritual of the ancient Parsees, or fire worshippers, and eclipsing the very clouds of heaven in their gigantic wreath of incense. And a strange, wild, savage music seems to accompany these loud litanies; bell and ball, hammer and shears, crank and chains, wheels and rolls, steam, blast and engine screams, yell and howl, and shriek and roar and hiss, and above them all, the big shout of the forgeman, or call of the collier, seems ever and anon to set them on yelling, howling, shrieking, roaring, and hissing with a renewed grim energy, as if they were resolved to deafen every other tone of mortal sound except their own hideous minstrelsy. And when the mild, quiet moon looks down at times upon the riot, like a ' blue light' on a field of fireworks, so stillness looks more still in the contrast of the rioting, and she seems timidly to steal away faster than usual through the mountain masses of drifting smoke clouds, that irreverently smoke in her face as if she was a common street lamp. The stranger shudders as he beholds the scene. Far as the eye can reach it is a series of fires ; there seems to be too much fire and too much fury to be ever put out again. The dread is that it must grow and spread beyond its flaming boundaries, till the whole realm be in a general blaze, which all its island waters cannot quench, and bonny England become a holocaust."

The population during the last half century has been rapidly increasing, as is evident from the following statement :—

| | | | | |
|---|---|---|---|---|
| 1801 | . | . | . | . 4,160 |
| 1811 | . | . | . | 5,372 |
| 1821 | . | . | . | . 6,471 |
| 1831 | . | . | . | 8,437 |
| 1841 | . | . | . | . 11,025 |
| 1851 | . | . | . | 14,278 |

The parish is in the West Bromwich Union, but there being no union workhouse, the poor are provided for in a house set apart for this purpose. The Rev. W. G. Cole, B.A., incumbent of S. James's, is chaplain.

L

The means at present used for the conveyance of goods and passengers are remarkable as contrasted with those formerly in vogue. The old pack horse and stage coach travelling have been superseded by the modern improvements of railroads and canals, there being three lines of railway running through the parish, viz., the London and North Western, the South Staffordshire, and the Birmingham, Wolverhampton, and Dudley, with a station for each, besides branches of the Birmingham Canal. The survey for the canal from Wednesbury to Birmingham was first made in the year 1782, by R. Whitworth, " it being supposed that the intended canal would communicate with upwards of 2,000 acres of Wednesbury coals, worth, according to the thickness, and situation of the mine, from £160 to £250 per acre, above the expense of getting the coal, *for which there was no market.* Moreover large quantities of Wednesbury coals were carried into Oxfordshire and other counties, *by land carriage*, at a great expense, whereas by canal they could be procured at much easier rates." The saving at Oxford is reckoned as follows :—

| | £ | s. | d. | | £ | s. | d. |
|---|---|---|---|---|---|---|---|
| Wednesbury coal at the pits, per ton | 0 | 3 | 8 | Present average price of pit coal, at Oxford, per ton . | 1 | 13 | 4 |
| Tonnage to Barn Close, near Birmingham . . . | 0 | 1 | 2 | | | | |
| Tonnage from thence to Oxford, 128 miles, at 1d. per ton per mile . . . | 0 | 10 | 8 | | | | |
| Freight from Wednesbury to Oxford, ¾d. per ton per mile . | 0 | 8 | 7½ | | | | |
| | | | | | 1 | 4 | 1½ |
| | 1 | 4 | 1½ | Reduction in the price at Oxford, per ton | 0 | 9 | 2½ |

It appears from the evidence given in the report of Thos. Webster Rammell, Esq., Superintendent Inspector of the General Board of Health, who visited the town in March, 1851, that " there are three turnpike trusts within the parish—the Bilston, Birmingham, and Walsall. They do not any of them pass through the town, the several Acts of Parliament prohibiting them. The whole of the town roads were repaired by the surveyors of the highways previous to the establishment of the Board of Health. The total length of the parish roads is 13¼ miles. The actual amount of highway rates collected for five years will be seen from the following table :—

|  |  |  | £ | s. | d. |
|---|---|---|---|---|---|
| 1846, 3d. in the pound | . | . | . 347 | 18 | 11 |
| 1847, 5d. in the pound | . | . | 547 | 19 | 8¼ |
| 1848, 3d. in the pound | . | . | . 336 | 3 | 9¼ |
| 1849, 5d. in the pound | . | . | 544 | 1 | 4 |
| 1850, 4d. in the pound | . | . | . 463 | 17 | 10¼ |
|  |  |  | 2240 | 1 | 7¼ |

According to the above-mentioned report, " the number of inhabited houses in 1841 was 2146; uninhabited, 97; building, 19." It also gives the following return of the number and rateable value of houses and other property at present in the parish, showing an increase of nearly 500 houses to have taken place within the last ten years.

The number of rateable houses upon the undermentioned amounts, viz. :—

|  |  |  |  |  |  |  |
|---|---|---|---|---|---|---|
| Not exceeding £2 | | | . | . | . | 12 |
| Above £2 | ,, | 3 | . | . | . | 180 |
| ,, 3 | ,, | 4 | . | . | . | 317 |
| ,, 4 | ,, | 5 | . | . | . | 616 |
| ,, 5 | ,, | 6 | . | . | . | 518 |

| | | | | | | |
|---|---|---|---|---|---|---|
| Above £6, and not exceeding £10 | | . | . | | | 705 |
| „ 10 | „ | 15 | . | . | . | 170 |
| „ 15 | „ | 20 | | . | | 78 |
| „ 20 | „ | 30 | . | . | . | 73 |
| „ 30 | „ | 40 | | . | . | 16 |
| „ 40 | „ | 50 | . | . | . | 16 |
| „. 50 | „ | 80 | . | | . | 9 |

Total number of houses    .    . 2710

| | £ | s. | d. |
|---|---|---|---|
| Rateable value of the above houses is  . | 20,450 | 9 | 0 |
| Rateable value of the works, pits, and manufactories  .   .   . | 6,844 | 7 | 0 |
| Rateable value of land  .   .  . | 3,706 | 0 | 0 |
| Birmingham Canal Company  .   . | 453 | 0 | 0 |
| Birmingham and Staffordshire Gas Company  .  .   .   .   . | 54 | 10 | 0 |
| South Staffordshire Railway Company  . | 262 | 10 | 0 |
| London and North Western Railway Company .  .  . .   .   . | 85 | 0 | 0 |
| Rateable value of the whole, one rate . | 31,855 | 16 | 0 |

The gross estimated rental will be 10 per cent. higher than the rateable value upon buildings, and 5 per cent. higher upon lands. The rural district of the Delves comprises 600 acres of land; the number of houses is 26, with 135 inhabitants.

Although Wednesbury occupies an important position among the manufacturing parishes of South Staffordshire, yet, as with the majority of such localities, no attention has been paid until of late to the comfort and cleanliness of the dwellings of the inhabitants. No provision was made for the paving, lighting, and draining of the town, any more than for a good supply of water. Mr. Rammell remarks that

" the natural sources of water have mostly failed and been
diminished, by reason of the mining operations carried on
in the parish and neighbourhood, consequently the inhabitants suffer a want almost amounting to destitution in regard
to this important element, having to send, in many instances,
a great distance to procure it, and at a very considerable
expense. The poorer people are generally obliged to use
water lying in stagnant pools, filthy and unwholesome in the
extreme for most domestic purposes, being unable to procure
a better supply. The consequence of this scarcity of water
is that the dwellings of the poor are unavoidably dirty, and
as they are generally small and badly constructed, closely
packed together, without drainage of any sort, and ill-venti-
lated, epidemics, endemics, and contagious diseases prevail
at all times in Wednesbury. The cholera in 1832 and in
1849 committed fearful ravages, 90 dying of this fearful
disease in 1832, and 218 in 1849. The mortality for many
years has been very high, the average of the seven years
ending Michaelmas, 1849, being after the rate of 26½ in
1000; whilst that since Michaelmas, 1849, has been
much heavier, there having been 198 deaths in the eleven
weeks ending March 18, 1851, being at the enormous rate of
62 per 1000 per annum." From this continuous and alarming
increase in the average ratio of mortality, it became obvious
to all that some steps must be taken to improve the general
condition of the town, consequently a petition signed by more
than one-tenth of the rated inhabitants was presented to the
General Board of Health, praying for an inquiry into the
sanitary condition of the parish, with a view to the application of the Public Health Act. A commissioner, T. W.
Rammell, Esq., was sent down by the Board, who entered
upon the inquiry on the 19th of March, 1851, and published

his report, before alluded to, in June following.  The result was an order in Council, bearing date the 26th day of December, 1851, appointing the Reverend Isaac Clarkson " to exercise the powers and perform the duties vested in or imposed upon the Chairman of the Local Board of Health, by the Public Health Act, 1848, in relation to the first election by owners of property and ratepayers, and to perform all other duties requisite to be performed in conducting the first election of members of the Local Board of Health for the parish of Wednesbury."  The election was accordingly proceeded with, and the requisite number of persons chosen. The Board thus constituted sits every alternate Monday, and has already done something towards the improvement of the town, inasmuch as the greater part of it is now lighted with gas, the lodging-houses are better regulated, many nuisances have been removed, and attention paid to the building and arrangement of all new houses in course of erection.  A plan of the parish has been prepared by the Surveyor to the Board, Mr. T. W. Fereday, of Wolverhampton, and it is hoped that a thorough system of draining, with a good supply of water, will speedily follow.

It is much to be feared that the morals and religion of the inhabitants of Wednesbury, in days gone by, were as little attended to as the sanitary condition of the place.  The unenviable notoriety it has gained in the annals of bull-baiting, cock-fighting, and other low and brutal amusements leads to this conclusion, and points to the generation just passed away as one Godless and desperately wicked.  The population was suffered to increase, and no additional churches provided, neither were schools to be found for the education of the young,—and hence the evil lives of the people.  Happily the case is different *now ;* and it is mainly owing to the exertions of the present vicar that Wednesbury is so well supplied with church accommodation and schools.

We now proceed to give an account of the new churches and schools according to the date of erection, commencing with

## S. John's Church.

IN the year 1843 an act was passed, (6 and 7 Vict. c. 37,) intituled " An Act to make better Provision for the Spiritual Care of Populous Parishes," and commonly called " Sir Robert Peel's Act," of which the vicar, the Rev. I. Clarkson, immediately took advantage, and caused the parish of Wednesbury to be divided in such a manner as to constitute three new ecclesiastical districts, viz. :—S. John's, S. James's, and Moxley, reserving the larger proportion of the population to the parish church.

S. John's was formed into an ecclesiastical district in the year 1844, and the Rev. John Winter, M.A., appointed the perpetual curate, by the Crown. Divine service was celebrated in a licensed room until the church was built.

The first encouragement given to the erection of the church was a promise made by the late E. T. Foley, Esq., to endow it with a moiety of the great tithes of the whole parish.

The site was given by the late Samuel Addison, Esq., in addition to £500 to the building fund, and £700 for the completion of the spire. The foundation stone was laid by Lady Emily Foley, on Thursday, March the 27th, 1845, and the church consecrated by the Lord Bishop of the Diocese on Wednesday, May 13, 1846. The sermon at the consecration was preached by the Rev. Isaac Clarkson, from 2 Chron. vi. 41—" Now therefore arise, O Lord God, into

Thy resting place, Thou and the ark of Thy strength," &c.
On the following Sunday the sermons were preached by the
Revs. J. H. Sharwood, M.A., and J. B. Owen, M.A. The
collections at the consecration and on the Sunday following
amounted to £115 19s. 2d.

The church is built of stone, in the Early English style
of architecture, having a capacious and lofty nave, surmounted by a clerestory, with an open timber roof; north
and south aisles; and a high and elegant tower and spire,
facing the main street. The whole area of the nave is
occupied by open seats. The chancel is lighted by a triple
lancet window, having deep and richly ornamented arches,
supported by columns, with floriated heads. The font (the
gift of the architects) is placed at the north entrance, and is
in accordance with the style of the church. An organ has
lately been presented by James Bagnall and Thomas Walker,
Esqs.; it is unfortunately placed so as to block up the
principal door, but it has led to the removal of an ugly
gallery. Gas has lately been introduced into the church,
but the fittings, being after the similitude of those used in
shops and such like buildings, are very unsightly. The
church contains one thousand sittings—one half of which
are free. The architects were Messrs. Daukes and Hamilton;
the builder—Mr. Isaac Highway, of Walsall. It appears to
have been more in accordance with the taste of the builders
to place the church on a line with the street, than to adhere
to the universal custom of having it due east and west.

The cost of the church (including the site, tower, and
spire) was £5,758 6s. 4d. This sum was raised by grants
from the Lichfield Diocesan Church Extension Society (of
£920), from the Incorporated Society for Building Churches
and Chapels (of £400), and the remainder by voluntary

contributions. The carpet within the altar rails was presented by Mrs. Elwell, of Wood Green; the linen for the communion table by Mrs. Fletcher, of Dudley; and the books for the minister by the Society for Promoting Christian Knowledge.

The living is a perpetual curacy, value £300, the church being endowed by £150 per annum by the Ecclesiastical Commissioners, under the Act of the 6th and 7th Victoria, and with the moiety of the great tithes of the whole parish of Wednesbury. The pew rents are paid to the incumbent, (less £6 per annum given by the churchwardens to the clerk), as also Easter offerings, according to ancient custom, the vicar's claim to these having ceased when the church was consecrated. The living is in the patronage of Lady Emily Foley; E. T. Foley, Esq. dying before the deed conveying his moiety of the great tithes was executed, his widow, the Lady Emily Foley, fulfilled his pious intention on the 6th of August, 1847, in consideration of which the Queen, in Council, August 16th, 1847, granted to the Right Honourable Lady Emily Foley, her heirs and assigns for ever, the right of patronage of the new parish of S. John the Evangelist, and the nomination of the perpetual curate thereof. The present incumbent is the Rev. John Winter, M.A.; curate, the Rev. ——— Devis, B.A., who succeeded the Rev. Alfred Jones, B.A. Churchwardens, Messrs. Thomas Walker and Thomas Bill. The hours of Divine service are —on Sunday half-past ten, three, and half-past six; and on Wednesday evening at seven o'clock. The following inscription is on a tablet inside the church :—

Sacred to the memory of John Wood, one of the first wardens of this parish, who departed this life July 9th, 1847, in the 45th year of his age. His amiable and generous disposition attracted universal

M

esteem. This monument was erected in affectionate remembrance of one of the best of fathers, by his eldest son, James Wood.

In the midst of life we are in death.

S. John's Parish Schools were built in the years 1848-9, at a cost of £1,158 10s. 2d. (including the fittings and £123 15s. paid for the site), and were opened on the 11th of March, 1849. They are nicely built, and afford accommodation for 300 scholars; they are used for Sunday as well as daily schools. The Committee of Council on Education granted £321 to the building fund; the National Society, £225; and the Lichfield Diocesan Board, £25. The collections in the church at the opening of the schools were £100 5s. 2d.; and the sum of £487 5s. was raised by other voluntary contributions.

The population of this new parish is about 2,500, and consists principally of respectable householders, shop-keepers, coach smiths, ironworkers, miners, &c.

## S. James's Church.

S. James's, the second ecclesiastical district, was formed in the year 1844, from the lowest and most neglected part of the town, and numbers, in population, upwards of 3,000 souls, consisting chiefly of those who are employed in the mines, ironworks, and gas tube manufactories. When the district was constituted there existed no provision, in that portion of the town, for the maintenance of the worship of Almighty God, as prescribed by the Church, neither was there any place of worship at all, except a small Anabaptist meeting house in Dudley Street, the result of which was gross ignorance, spiritual destitution, and semi-barbarism.

The Rev. Joseph Hall, M.A., curate of the parish church, was appointed by the Crown to the perpetual curacy on the 22nd of September, 1844. He immediately commenced his pastoral visits, and although his undertaking was arduous and difficult, yet, in March, 1845, the new schools were opened and used for the celebration of Divine service, under a license from the Bishop, until the church was built.

The Rev. Joseph Hall resigned the incumbency May 21st, 1846; and was succeeded by the Rev. William Graham Cole, B.A., he having been presented to the living by the Bishop of the Diocese, on the 5th of September following.

On the 4th of January, 1847, a committee was formed for the purpose of making the necessary arrangements for building the new church; and on Wednesday, May 26th, 1847, the foundation stone was laid, Divine service having been celebrated in the parish church, and a sermon preached by the Rev. W. Dalton, M.A., Incumbent of S. Paul's, Wolverhampton, and Rural Dean. The offerings amounted to £38, and were applied to the building fund. A procession was formed from the parish church to the intended site, and the foundation stone laid by Thomas Bagnall, Esq., of Great Barr, chairman of the building committee, in the presence of a large concourse of people. The church was consecrated by the Lord Bishop of the Diocese on Wednesday, May 31, 1848. The sermon was preached by his lordship from Luke iv. 18. "To preach the Gospel to the poor." On the following Sunday, June 4th, the sermons were preached by the Rev. W. Dalton, B.D.; the Rev. J. C. Barrett, M.A., Incumbent of S. Mary's, Birmingham; and the Rev. Henry Bagnall, M.A., Rector of Sheinton, and Rural Dean of Condover, Salop. The sum collected at the offertory, on the day of consecration, and on the Sunday, including the

Bishop's ancient fee of £6 13s. 4d., presented by his lordship, amounted to £194 19s. 11d.

The church consists of a nave 70 feet by 48 feet 3 inches, with open roof, filled in with ornamental timber. The chancel is 22 feet by 12 feet, the vestry and porch each being on one side. The tower is 65 feet high, with embattled top, surmounted by four octagonal pinnacles. There is a gallery at the west end of the church, in which is placed the organ. The font stands near the west door, and the eagle lectern on the south side of the chancel arch; on the north side is the pulpit, which formerly belonged to the parish church of Kidderminster. The church is well lighted with gas, the fittings having been presented by Messrs. James Russell and Sons. The altar cloth and linen, used at the administration of the Holy Communion, were given by the ministers and churchwardens; also some additional vessels have since been presented for the Holy Table. The service books were the gift of the Society for Promoting Christian Knowledge.

The church contains 855 sittings, 566 of which are free and unappropriated for ever; it was erected at a cost (including the site) of £3,305 17s. 3d. To meet this sum grants were made, of £850 by the Lichfield Diocesan Church Extension Society; of £500 by the Ecclesiastical Commissioners; of £450 by the Incorporated Society for Building Churches and Chapels; of £250 placed at the disposal of the Ecclesiastical Commissioners by the late Sir Robert Peel, Bart.; and the remainder was raised by voluntary contributions.

The church is very plain, indeed it is a matter of surprise that, in these days of revived art, such a building as it is should have been erected at all. One strictly architectural would have cost no more than this, which can be ranked under no ecclesiastical style whatever.

The living is a perpetual curacy, in the patronage of the Crown and the Bishop alternately, and of the yearly value of about £180. The pew rents and Easter offerings are received by the incumbent, less £6 per annum out of the former, which the churchwardens are authorised to pay to the clerk of the church.

There is an excellent parsonage house close to the church and schools, erected in the years 1849-50. The cost of the building (including £105 paid for the site) was £1,043 12s. 10d. This amount was raised by a grant of £200 from the Governors of Queen Anne's Bounty; by a loan of £200 from the same; by a further grant of £200 from the Lichfield Diocesan Church Extension Society; and the remainder by voluntary contributions.

The present incumbent is the Rev. William Graham Cole, B.A.; curates, Rev. Richard Twigg, and the Rev. W. B. Flowers, B.A., who succeeded the Rev. F. P. B. N. Hutton, B.A. Churchwardens, John Nock Bagnall and William Sutton Nayler. Sidesmen, John Smith and Richard Hayes. Hours of Divine service—daily, at half-past seven in the evening. On Sundays, at half-past ten, three, and half-past six.

S. James's Schools were erected, as we have already stated, immediately after the district was constituted, and opened in March, 1845. The cost of the building was £1,126 19s. This sum includes the site, the residence of the master and mistress, and the fittings necessary for the celebration of Divine service. The building fund was provided by grants and voluntary contributions. The grants were—£359 from the Committee of Council on Education, £330 from the

National Society, and £30 from the Pastoral Aid Society.
The collections at the opening were £29 18s. 6d. These
schools will accommodate 80 boys, 80 girls, and 90 infants,
and are used for the purpose of Daily and Sunday Schools.

## Moxley Church.

Moxley, the third ecclesiastical district, was formed in the
year 1845, from portions of the parishes of Wednesbury, Darlaston, and Bilston, and contains a population of about 3000
souls, chiefly composed of miners, and persons employed in
the manufacture of iron. The Rev. Thomas Knight. M.A.,
was appointed by the Crown to the perpetual curacy.

There is a large school room in this parish, capable of
holding 160 children, also a house for the clergyman and
the master, built in the years 1837-8, at a cost of £1,100,
raised by subscription. The room has been used for Divine
worship, as well as for a daily and Sunday school, until the
consecration of the church.

The Rev. Thomas Knight resigned the incumbency, on the
11th of August, 1847, and was succeeded by the Rev. Patrick
Wilson, M.A., who received his appointment from the
Bishop of Lichfield, on the 14th of October, 1847.

The foundation stone of the new church, dedicated to
" All Saints," was laid on Friday, May 3rd, 1850, by the
Lady Emily Foley, Divine service having been previously
celebrated in the school room. The prayers were said by
the Rev. G. W. White, M.A., Rector of Darlaston, and the
sermon preached by the Rev. W. Dalton, B.D. ; after which
a collection was made, when the offerings amounted to £32.

The church was consecrated on Friday, June 27th, 1851.
At the consecration, after a sermon by the Lord Bishop of

the Diocese, £26 7s. 2d. were collected; and on the following
Sunday, after sermons by the Revs. G. Fisk, W. Crump,
and J. Y. Rooker, the collections amounted to £25 9s.
Unfortunately, All Saints' Church, Moxley, although somewhat better than the sister church of S. James, is still far
from being what it should be, as to its architecture. It
appears to be built after a style of the architect's own, in a
great measure; and although there are some who delight to
call it " Early English," we feel certain that beautiful and
elegant style will not own this paltry modern incongruity.
The church contains 635 sittings, 446 of which are free for
ever. To complete the whole, about £3,000 are required;
but, owing to a considerable deficiency in the funds, the
erection of the spire is at present deferred. The following
grants have been made to this church :—The Lichfield Diocesan Church Extension Society, £635 ; the Ecclesiastical
Commissioners for England, £500 ; the Church Commissioners, £260 ; the Incorporated Society for Building
Churches and Chapels, £250 ; £500 from the Wolverhampton Deanery Fund; and £50 from " the Peel
Memorial" Fund.

The living is in the patronage of the Crown and the
Bishop of Lichfield alternately.

## The Delves Chapel.

The Delves is an agricultural district, situated two miles
from the parish church of Wednesbury, and contains about
160 inhabitants. For the spiritual benefit of this too long
neglected people, a small chapel has been erected by voluntary contributions. The foundation stone was laid by the

Rev. I. Clarkson, and the building completed at a cost of
£315. It was opened for Divine service, under license from
the Bishop of the Diocese, on the 13th of September, 1850.
The morning sermon was preached by the Rev. R. Hawes,
M.A., Curate of Walsall; and that in the afternoon by the
Rev. I. Clarkson; £19 11s. were collected. The chapel has
accommodation for 100 persons.

## King's Hill Chapel.

King's Hill is a part of the parish of Wednesbury, close
to the town of Darlaston, containing a population of colliers,
miners, artisans, &c. In 1851 it was determined to erect
a small chapel for this part of the parish, and thus provide
in some measure for the spiritual welfare of the 2,000 souls
living there. The building was erected at a cost of about
£400, and opened for Divine Service on the 11th of May,
1851. The Rev. Henry Taylor is Curate of the Delves and
King's Hill.

It is pleasing to reflect that every part of the parish is
now supplied with a church or chapel in connexion with the
Church of England, wherein the people may worship God
after the manner of their forefathers, and that the Gospel is
brought to the very doors of the inhabitants. A few years
ago there was but one church for the whole parish; now
there are four, and two chapels, and fourteen services every
Sunday; we wish we could add that each church has its
daily service, but in this respect Wednesbury is sadly
wanting, S. James's being the only parish where the church
is open for the worship of God every day. Not fifty years
ago, there were regularly two services, every Wednesday and

Friday, and also on every day appointed by the Church to be kept holy, in the Old Church; but it is much to be regretted that this good custom has of late fallen into desuetude.

The Market Place is in the centre of the town and occupies about an acre of land. Here stood formerly the ancient cross, usually erected in such situations, in order to inculcate upright intentions and fairness of dealing. Many beautiful market crosses still remain in the country, and happily, instead of being destroyed, they are now being restored to their pristine beauty. Previous to the demolition of the Wednesbury Market Cross, a school was kept there, for the education of twelve boys and eight girls; but it has been discontinued about fifty years.

The original grant of a market here was made by Queen Anne to John Hoo, of Bradley, Esq., Serjeant-at-law. The following is a copy of the charter :—

*Third part of Patents in y⁰ 7th year of y⁰ reign of Queen Anne.—A grant to John Hoo, Esq.*

𝕿𝖍𝖊 𝕼𝖚𝖊𝖊𝖓. To all to whom, &c. greeting.—Whereas it appears by a certain inquisition indented, taken at y⁰ parish of King's Swinford, in our county of Stafford, the 24th day of May, in y⁰ 7th year of our reign, before James Wood, Esq,. sheriff of the county aforesaid, by virtue of our certain writ of " Ad quod damnum," to y⁰ said sheriff directed, and to y⁰ inquisition aforesaid annexed, by y⁰ oath of good and lawful men of y⁰ county aforesaid, that it would not be to y⁰ damage or injury of us, or of any others, if we should grant to our beloved and faithful John Hoo, of Bradley, in y⁰ county aforesaid, Esq., serjeant-at-law, license that he and his heirs might have and hold, at Wednesbury, otherwise Wedgebury, in y⁰ county aforesaid, *two fairs* or *marts*, yearly, for ever (that is to say), one of y⁰ said fairs upon y⁰ 25th of April, and y⁰ other on y⁰ 23rd of July, unless either of the aforesaid days should be Sunday, and then upon y⁰ Monday next following such Sunday, for y⁰ buying and selling of all and all manner of cattle and beasts, and of all and all manner of goods, wares, and merchandizes commonly bought and sold in fairs or marts. And also one market on Friday in every week, for ever, for buying and selling corn, flesh and fish, and other provision, and all and all manner of goods, wares, and merchandizes, commonly bought and sold in markets. And further, by the inquisition aforesaid, it appears that it would not be to yᵉ damage or injury of us, or of others, or to yᵉ hurt of neighbouring markets or fairs, if we should grant to the aforesaid John Hoo, license that he and his heirs might have and hold yᵉ fairs or marts, and markets aforesaid, at Wednesbury, otherwise Wedgebury aforesaid, in manner and form aforesaid, as by yᵉ said writ and inquisition remaining of record in yᵉ files of our Chancery more fully doth and may appear. Now, know ye, that we, of our especial grace, and of our certain knowledge and mere motion, have given and granted, and by these presents, for us, our heirs and successors, do give and grant to yᵉ aforesaid John Hoo and his heirs, free and lawful power, license, and authority, that he or they, and every of them, may, from henceforth, for ever, have, hold, and keep, at Wednesbury, otherwise Wedgebury aforesaid, two fairs or marts, yearly, for ever (that is to say), one of yᵉ said fairs on yᵉ 25th of April, and yᵉ other on yᵉ 23rd of July, unless either of yᵉ aforesaid days shall be Sunday, and then upon yᵉ Monday next following such Sunday, for yᵉ buying and selling of all and all manner of cattle and beasts, and all and all manner of goods, wares, and merchandizes, commonly bought and sold in fairs or marts ; and also one market on Friday in every week, for ever, for yᵉ buying and selling of corn, flesh, and fish, and other provisions, and all and all manner of goods, wares, and merchandizes, commonly bought and sold in markets ; together with courts of pie poudre at yᵉ time and times of yᵉ aforesaid fairs ; and with reasonable tolls, tollage, piccage, and stallage for cattle, goods, merchandize, and wares to be sold, or exposed for sale, in the fair and markets aforesaid, to have, hold, and enjoy yᵉ aforesaid fairs or marts, and markets, and courts of pie poudre,* piccage, and stallage, and premises above, by these presents, granted or mentioned, to be granted to yᵉ said John Hoo and his heirs, for ever, to yᵉ only and proper use and behoof of yᵉ said John Hoo, his heirs and

---

* A court held in fairs to yield justice to buyers and sellers, and for redress of all disorders committed in them ; and so called because it is usually held in summer, and the suitors commonly are country people, with dusty feet : or from the expedition intended in hearing of causes proper thereunto, before the dust goes off the plaintiff's and defendant's feet.

assigns, for ever, and this without any account, or any other thing, to be
therefore rendered, paid, or done to us, our heirs, or successors. Where-
fore, we will, and by these presents, for us, our heirs and successors, firmly
enjoyning, do order and command that y⁸ aforesaid John Hoo, his heirs and
assigns, and every of them, shall, by virtue of these presents, well, freely,
lawfully, and quietly, have, hold, and keep, and may and shall be able to
have, hold, and keep for ever, y⁸ aforesaid fair and markets, and courts of
pie poudre, tolls, tollage, piccage, and stallage, and other y⁸ premises aforesaid, according to y⁸ true intent of these, our letters patent, without
y⁸ molestation, disturbance, hindrance, or contradiction of us, our heirs or
successors, or of any sheriff, escheators, bailiff's officer, or minister, of us,
our heirs or successors whatsoever, and this without any other warrant, writ,
or process to be hereafter procured or obtained in that behalf. And
further, we will, and by these presents, for us, our heirs and successors, do
grant to the aforesaid John Hoo and his heirs, that these our letters
patent, on y⁸ enrollment thereof, may and shall be good, firm, valid and
sufficient and effectual in law, for the said John Hoo and his heirs according to y⁸ true intent of the same.

In witness whereof, etc.

Witness the QUEEN, at Westminster, 9th of July, by Writ of Privy
Seal, 1709.

Although this charter gives but one market day (Friday),
another was established, on the Saturday, about thirty years
ago. Both markets are well supplied with everything except
live stock, and are frequented, not only by the people of the
town, but by the inhabitants of Darlaston, Tipton, and West
Bromwich. A heavy toll is paid to the lord of the manor.
The tolls are at present let for £60 a year.

About a century and half since a Quaker's meeting house
was built in High Street. It was erected by the Fidoe
family, who also gave the site ; adjoining the meeting house
was also a burial ground, where many of the "Friends" were
interred. The South Staffordshire Railway passes through
this ground, in the cutting of which many human bones were

exhumed. Owing to the Society of Friends being so reduced in numbers, they have long since ceased to use this place, and hold no meetings in the parish. In 1820 it was converted into a school, under the Lancasterian system; subsequently it became a cooperage; but is used again as a school.

We have already noticed the principal public buildings in the preceding pages; in addition to these there are the following meeting houses belonging to Protestant denominations, viz. :—two Wesleyan, one Anabaptist, two Primitive Methodist, one New Connexion, one Independent, and one Reformed Wesleyan. A Popish " place of worship" has lately been erected adjacent to the parish church. The Wesleyans also have a large school. There is a Town Hall used as a public office, where petty sessions are held every Tuesday; adjoining which is the police station, with cells underneath.

The principal trades of Wednesbury are the manufacture of patent gas tubes, merchant bars, hoops, sheets, boiler-plates, railway bars, patent shafts, axles and wheels, edge tools, spades, coach springs, hinges, screws, files, &c., and all kinds of cast iron articles. During the late war, the staple articles produced at Wednesbury were gunlocks, of which immense quantities were sent weekly to Birmingham, for the use of the musket manufacturer. Very high wages were obtained for the forging and filing of these locks before the general peace, but they subsequently fell as much as 70 per cent. The workmen suffered greatly from this reduction, and in their distress petitioned Parliament to do something for them. Mr. Littleton (now Lord Hatherton) presented the petition, and supported the prayer. Although this trade did not again flourish to so great an extent as formerly, yet others were introduced, and the parish is in a more prosperous condition than ever. Wednesbury has been long celebrated for its valuable coal and ironstone mines, but especially for the former. The coal and iron trades being of so much importance to the welfare of the place, the following chapter is devoted to a short account of them, having, however, especial reference to Wednesbury.

# CHAPTER VI.

## Coal and Iron.

———

It is a question often discusssed, whether the ancient Britons had any knowledge of the coal so abundantly discovered in later times. Whitaker, the historian of Manchester, is of opinion that the primæval Britons used coal. He argues, first, from the probability of their discovering it in those parts of the country where, as at Wednesbury, the extremities of the strata appear through the earth, and are exposed to view ; he brings also the name of this fuel itself as a further proof of his assertion, affirming that the word " coal" is of British, not Saxon origin. By certain undoubted facts, however, lately brought to light, conjecture yields to actuality. A few years since, several pieces of coal were found in the sand under the Roman road leading to Ribchester. We are further told by Pennant, in his *Tour in Wales*, that a *flint axe*, an instrument commonly in use amongst the aborigines of our island, was discovered firmly fixed in a certain vein of coal which was exposed to view in Craig-y-Larc, in Monmouthshire, and in a situation easy to be got at by men unskilled in mining. "The Romans," says Whitaker, "appear continually using coal in Britain. In the West Riding of Yorkshire are many beds of cinders, heaped up in the fields, in one of which a number of coins was found some years ago." Horseley, in the *Britannia Romana*, remarks that, at Benwell, near New-castle-upon-Tyne, there was a "coalry" near that place, which is judged by those who are best skilled in such affairs to have been wrought by the Romans. It is also the opinion of Wallis *(History of Northumberland)* that "the Romans were as well acquainted with our *pit coal* as with our *ores* and *metals*; in digging up some of the foundation of their walled city Magna, or Caervorran, in 1762, coal cinders, some very large, were turned up, which glowed in the fire like other cinders, and were not to be known from them when taken out." Towards the middle of the ninth century we find ourselves on less doubtful ground; Whitaker mentions a grant made A.D. 853, of some lands by the Abbey of Peterborough, by which certain payments in kind were reserved to the monastery, among others we find sixty cart-loads of wood, and twelve of *fossil* or pit coal, which proves, it would seem, that coal was known and used by the Saxons in Britain.

Concerning the early working of mines in Wednesbury there can be no doubt; it has long been celebrated for the prime quality of its coal, which is deservedly preferred on account of its suitableness to domestic purposes, and to the making, smelting, and manufacturing of iron. The rise of the neighbouring town of Birmingham has been attributed to its vicinity to the mines of Wednesbury.  Hutton, the historian of Birmingham, thus writes on the subject:* "We know the instruments of war used by the Britons were a sword, spear, shield, and scythe.  If they were not the manufacturers, how came they by these instruments?  We cannot allow that either they, or the chariots were imported, because that will give them a much greater consequence. They must have been well acquainted with the tools used in husbandry, for they were masters of the field in a double sense.  Bad, also, as their houses were, a chest of carpenter's tools would be necessary to complete them.  We cannot doubt, from these evidences, and others which might be adduced, that the Britons understood the manufacture of iron.

"Perhaps history cannot produce an instance of an improving country, like England, where the coarse manufacture of iron has been carried on, that ever that laborious art went to decay, except the materials failed; and as we know of no place where such materials have failed, there is the utmost reason to believe our forefathers, the Britons, were supplied with those necessary implements by the black artists of the Birmingham forge.  Ironstone and coal are the materials for this production, both of which are found in the neighbourhood in great plenty.  The two following circumstances strongly evince this ancient British manufactory: —Upon the borders of the parish (Birmingham) stands Aston Furnace, appropriated for melting ironstone, and reducing it into pigs; this has the appearance of great antiquity.  From the melted ore, in this subterranean region of infernal aspect, is produced a calx, or cinder, of which there is an enormous mountain.  From an attentive

* We do not profess to agree with the *whole* of Mr. Hutton's theory.

survey the observer would suppose so prodigious a heap could not accumulate in one hundred generations ; however, it shows no perceptible addition in the age of man. There is also a common of vast extent, called Wednesbury Old Field, in which are the vestiges of many hundred coal pits, long in disuse, which the curious antiquarian would deem as long in sinking, as the mountain of cinders in rising. The minute sprig of Birmingham, no doubt, first took root in this black soil, which, in a succession of ages, has grown to its present opulence. At what time this prosperous plant was set, is very uncertain ; perhaps as long before the days of Cæsar as it is since. Thus the mines of Wednesbury empty their riches into the lap of Birmingham, and thus she draws nurture from the bowels of the earth."

The same author brings the road leading from Wednesbury to Birmingham as an additional evidence of the ancient working of the mines in the former place. He says, " When an ancient road led up an eminence it was worn by the long practice of ages into a deep holloway, some of which were twelve or fourteen yards below the surface of the banks, with which they were once even, and so narrow as to admit only one passenger. . . . . Some of these no doubt were formed by the spade, to soften the fatigue of climbing the hill, but many were owing to the pure efforts of time, the horse and the showers." Several of these holloways still retain their name, thereby marking their origin, and amongst them we notice the Holloway Bank, near Wednesbury, over which it is conjectured the produce of the Wednesbury mines was carried on horses' backs to Aston Furnace and Birmingham.

The antiquity of the mining operations in this parish is confirmed by the fact of the mines coming to the surface in many parts; and the name of "the Delves," given to a portion of it, may be considered a further proof. Some years ago, a square shaft was discovered there. Tradition calls such pits as these "Dane's shafts," and applies the appellation of "Dane's cinders" to certain large heaps of scoria, met with in many places in England, with so great an accumulation of soil as to grow trees of a large size. Dud Dudley, in his *Metallum Martis*, mentions that, as early as 1665, "there were millions of tons of those cinders, and oaks growing upon them very old and rotten."

Dr. Wilkes, of Willenhall, produces an argument in favour of the early working of the mines, from the fact that the foundations of Wednesbury Church are laid with "pock-stone." In his time (1739) the fire in the pits had extended over many acres, which frequently burnt through to the surface, and by its great heat acted upon the strata above, according to their varied and peculiar natures. Some parts were reduced to cinders, others hardened to a very great degree. Clay thus hardened is here called "pock-stone," of which the roads about Wednesbury were almost entirely composed. The circumstance of the foundations of the church being formed of this kind of materials, is an evident proof that the Wednesbury collieries have been worked for several ages. The first actual mention of coal-pits in Wednesbury, as far as we have been able to discover, is in a deed, in the Record Office, Tower of London, entitled *Assignacio dotis Julianæ quæ fuit uxor Johannis de Heronville, &c.*, wherein a piece of land is described as "lying near Brades-walle, against the cole-pits." The date of this document is 1315.* The next account is taken from the *Itinerary* of

* This lady had also a share in a certain "iron mine," but where situated is not said.

Leland, the antiquary, who was employed by Henry VIII. to make a survey of England about the year 1538. He says, " There are secoles at Weddesbyrie, a village near Walsall.' Camden, who followed Leland, and wrote his *Britannia* about 1575, says, " The south part of Staffordshire hath coles, digged out of the earth, and mines of iron; but whether more to their commodity or hindrance, I leave to the inhabitants, who do or shall better understand it." The ancient parish registers also adduce evidence that the mines were worked in the days of Elizabeth. The register of burials, during that year, supplies instances of some who were killed whilst at work in the pits, amongst which is the following :—"*Anno* 1577, *Christopher Daly was buried; he was killed in the ryddinge, in the colepit.*" In the register of baptisms are the names of many children whose fathers are described as colliers and forgemen. In *The Proceedings in Chancery in the Reign of Queen Elizabeth,* is the record of a suit, as to whether the tenants of the manor of Wed- nesbury had a right to dig coals for their own use, they laying claim to the same. William Comberford, Esq., Lord of the Manor, was the plaintiff, and Elizabeth Nicholas and several others the defendants.

The best account of the working of the Wednesbury mines at the period when he wrote is to be found in Plot's *History of Staffordshire.* This curious book was published at Oxford in 1686, and the following account of the Wednesbury coal is here transcribed from it:—

" The smithy's and kitchen fires are much better supplied by the common coal of the country, especially that of Wed- nesbury, Dudley, and Sedgley, which some prefer to the Cannel itself; the texture and other qualities thereof being such, viz., that it is a flat, shining coal, having a pretty open grain, lying seldom in a level with the plane of the horizon, but most times somewhat inclining to it (according to which it cleaves into blocks at the discretion of the workmen), that it burns away with a sweet, bright flame, and into white ashes, leaving no such cinder as that from Newcastle-upon-Tyne; of which sort there is so great plenty in all parts of the county (especially about the three above-mentioned places) that most commonly there are twelve or fourteen collieries in work, and twice as many out of work, within ten miles round; some of which afford two thousand tons of coal yearly, others three, four, or five thousand. The upper beds, above the ironstone, lying sometimes ten, eleven, or twelve yards thick—nay, I was told by Mr. Pershouse, of Nether Gornall, that in his grounds at Ettingshall, in a place called Moorfields, the bed of coal is fourteen yards thick; insomuch that some acres of ground have been sold for £100 per acre. I was informed of one acre that sold for £150, and well indeed it might be so, for out of one single shaft there have been sometimes drawn £500 worth of coal. Nor indeed could the county well subsist without such vast supplies, the wood being most of it spent upon the iron works, for it is here (as well as in other countries that fetch their winter stores from hence) thought not only fit for the kitchen, but all other offices, even to the parlour and bedchamber; and not only in private families, but now, too, in most, if not all, the mechanic professions (except the iron works) that require the greatest expense of fuel, as the glass houses, salt works, brickmaking, and malting, all of which were heretofore performed with wood or charcoal, especially the last, which one would think should hardly admit of the unpleasant fumes of such firing; nor indeed does it, no more than of wood, for they have a way of charring it (if I may so speak) in all particulars as they do wood, whence the coal is freed from those noxious steams that would otherwise give the malt an ill odour. The coal thus prepared they call cokes, which conceives as strong a heat almost as charcoal itself, and is as fit for most other uses, but for malting, fining, and refining iron, *which it cannot be brought to do*, although attempted by the most skilful and curious artists. In the glass houses, salt works, and brick clamps they use the raw coal as brought from the pit; in the former I am not certain as to the proportion used, but in the Staffordshire Salt Works they use two tons to a drawing; and for burning a clamp of 16,000 bricks, they use seven tons of coal. The coal generally, in this and other countries, lies in the earth obliquely, *i. e.*, not perpendicular, but rising one way towards the surface of the earth, till it comes within a foot or two of the superfices, which the workmen generally call basetting, others cropping; and dipping into the earth the other way so deep, that it is seldom or ever followed to the end, or indeed anything near it (except where a mine lips or crops up again, as sometimes it does, as well in the dip as in the row); by reason the workmen are either prevented by water, or too deep a draught. This basseting or dipping is various, sometimes more and sometimes less; some dip not above 1 foot in 10, 20, or sometimes 30 feet; these they call flat mines, by reason of their evenness. The open works at Wednesbury seem to be of this kind, where there being but little earth lying over the measure of coal, the workmen rid off the earth, and dig the coal under their feet, and carry it out in wheelbarrows, there being no need for these of windlass, rope, or carf, whence these coal works are called foot rids or foot rills. In sinking for coal about Wednesbury, they meet with—first, earth and stone; second, blue clunch; and third, coal;

which is divided into the upper and lower coal. In the upper coal there are the following divisions, with their respective depths, &c. :—

|  |  | ft. | in. |  |
|---|---|---|---|---|
| 1.—The top or roof floor | . . . | 4 | 0 | thick. |
| 2.—Overslipper floor | . . . | 2 | 0 | ,, |
| 3.—Gay ditto | . . . | 2 | 0 | ,, |
| 4.—Lamb ditto | . . . | 2 | 0 | ,, |
| 5.—Kit ditto | . . . | 1 | 0 | ,, |
| 6.—Bench ditto | . . . | 2 | 6 | ,, |
| 7.—Spring ditto | . . . | 1 | 0 | ,, |
| 8.—Lower slipper ditto | . . . | 2 | 6 | ,, |

Then a bat between 1 and 3 yards thick which, being past, they come to the nether coal; which is divided as follows, viz. :—

|  |  | ft. | in. |  |
|---|---|---|---|---|
| 1.—The slip floor | . . . | 1 | 0 | ,, |
| 2.—Lam ditto | . . . | 2 | 0 | ,, |
| 3.—Oary ditto | . . . | 1 | 0 | ,, |
| 4.—Bench ditto | . . . | 1 | 0 | ,, |
| 5.—Spring ditto | . . . | 2 | 0 | ,, |
| 6.—Slipper ditto | . . . | 2 | 0 | ,, |

And then in 6 feet more they come to the ironstone.

" About Dudley, the three uppermost measures of coal are called the white measures; fourth, the shoulder coal; fifth, the toe coal; sixth, the foot coal; seventh, the yard coal; eighth, the slipper coal; ninth, the sawyer coal; tenth, the frisley coal; all which ten measures make up ten yards in thickness.

" In the working of the mine much inconvenience is experienced by the presence of damp; one sort is expelled either by water, or by letting down an iron cradle, they call their lamp, filled with fire, into the shaft or by the pit next to that they intend to work, which, making a draught, draws away the foul air. Another sort is expelled by a person entering the pit before the workmen, covered with wet sackcloth ; when he comes near where the damp is feared, he creeps on his belly with a long pole before him, having a lighted candle upon the top of it, which, coming in contact with the foul air, it explodes, and escapes by the mouth of the pit, the person that fired it escaping by creeping on the ground, keeping his face close to it till it is over. From the existence of these damps we may conclude that some coal pits may and do take fire of themselves, as it is unanimously agreed they do at Wednesbury (where the coal works now on fire take up eleven acres), Coseley, Etting-shall, and Pensnett, in this county, as Mr. Camden will have it, where he says a coal pit was fired by a candle, through the negligence of a groover ; and so possibly it might; but as for the rest, it is agreed they all fired of themselves, as they expect the shale and small coal in the old works will do, and have done, beyond all memory.

"For finding coal in a place where none has yet been discovered, they first consult the springs, if any be near, to see if they can find any water having a yellow sediment ; above ground they look for a smut, as they call it; when either of these are found they either bore or sink a pit ; if the coal lies shallow, the former is the better, but if deep, the latter, for the drawing the rods of the augre expending very much time, as there are many and must be often done, besides often leaving the searcher in great uncertainty as to the course of the coal, the draining it, its goodness, thick-ness, &c. ; whereas by sinking all these uncertainties are removed. The ordinary way they have of draining the mines is either by sough or by gin—the former when they have the advantage of fall of ground enough, which they try by the level. When they have no fall, they draw it up by gin, which is either bigger or less as required ; the less they call a jack, which is turned by men or horses as is necessary; but the gin is always worked by horses, which likewise is two-fold, either by chain or barrel; the chain is made with leather suckers upon it at little distances, which bring up water and discharge into a trough; the gin by barrel, whereof one always goes up as the other goes down, will raise great quantities of water if it be worked day and night, else, upon the least neglect, the water will get such a head, that much time will be spent before it can be mastered again."

This, then, is the account of the Wednesbury thick coal, at the close of the 17th century. The mode of working continued much the same until the latter half of the last century, when coal being applied to the manufacture of iron, such large quantities were required, and the demand became so great, that the steam engine was adapted to the purpose of draining the mines and raising the coal to the surface, by which means the bed of coal could be followed to almost its greatest depth.

One of the first engines erected by Savary was put up at Broadwaters, in the parish of Wednesbury. The following is Dr. Wilkes's account of it:—" Mr. Savary, the original inventor of the steam engine, set one down about the year 1739, near a place called ' Broadwaters,' in Wednesbury. This place being low ground, the water rose so hastily many years ago, and in such quantities from the coal pit, that it covered many acres of land, and buried many stacks of coal upon the bank. The engine there erected could not be brought to perfection, as the old pond of water was very great, and the springs in it many and strong, and the steam when too strong tore it all to pieces; so that after much time, labour, and expense, Mr. Savary gave up the undertaking, and the engine was laid aside as useless."

The old Wednesbury "thick coal" is now nearly exhausted; but other measures, lying deeper below the surface, are being worked. As the coal trade is so intimately con-nected with the iron trade in this district, we shall now proceed to give a short sketch of the rise and progress of the latter.

Various are the theories with regard to the first discovery of iron. Other metals were known and used before this, the most useful of all to mankind; but, nevertheless, in very early days, it was made serviceable to man, as is abundantly proved by many references to it in Sacred Writ. The name of Tubal Cain, the instructor of every artificer in brass and iron, is doubtless familiar to our readers; as also " the iron spear head" of Goliah, Og's iron bedstead, and the " bright iron in the market," spoken of by the prophet Ezekiel.

The Greeks and Romans were well acquainted with this useful metal, of which there is abundant proof. Upon Cæsar's invasion of Britain, B.C. 55, he found the people of this island well armed with swords, spears, and formidable war chariots, having scythes on the axles for cutting and tearing; and as it is certain the Britons of this period well understood the art of mining, it is but natural to suppose that they also knew and practised the art of ironmaking, and the manufacture of arms. The Romans, upon becoming conquerors of this island, established iron works in different parts, and they continued to work the iron mines until their final abandonment of Britain about A.D. 409 ; this is clearly demonstrated by the immense beds of cinders which have been discovered in many parts of the country in several instances, together with Roman coin and pottery; and furthermore, ruined altars, dedicated to *Jupiter Dolichenus*, the God of Iron Works, have also been found. A most interesting fact

P

is mentioned by Andrew Yarranton, in his book, *England's Improvement by Sea and Land,* published in 1698. He therein tells us, he himself saw dug up, near the walls of the city of Worcester, the hearth of one of the Roman foot blasts, which was seven feet deep in the ground, and by its side was an earthen vessel, containing about a peck of Roman coins.

The foot blast, here mentioned, was the ironmaking furnace of former days; it was an open hearth, upon which was placed alternately charcoal and ironstone, to which fire being applied, it was urged by men treading upon bellows. This operation was very slow and imperfect; unless the ore was very rich, not more than one cwt. of iron could be extracted in a day. The ironstone did not melt, but was found at the bottom of the hearth in a large lump or *bloom,* which was afterwards taken out and beaten under massive hammers, previous to its being worked into the required shape and form. The scoria, which was thrown on one side, contained more than one half iron, and these were the cinders, which, being found deep under ground (in some instances with oak trees of large proportions growing upon them), in after ages greatly enriched the proprietors of the soil; for, upon the introduction of the blast furnace, they were eagerly sought after, to work over again, as it was discovered they would make iron better for many purposes, and with less charcoal than ironstone did.

It would be difficult to attempt to form an accurate estimate of the extent of the iron trade, under this mode of manufacture, owing to the absence of authentic records. There is, however, a document quoted by Rudder, in his *History of Gloucestershire,* from which we learn that, in the tenth year of Edward I., 1282, there were in the Forest of

Dean 72 forges, called *moveable forges;* these probably could be carried from place to place, and hence their name. They paid annually to the King 7s. Henry II. granted to the Abbey of Flaxley two oaks out of the above forest every seven days, for the maintenance of a forge there. In the fourth year of Henry III., 1220, it was found by inquisition that the monks of Flaxley had a forge for making iron. The same year the itinerant Judges ordered that none should have a forge in the said Forest, without special license from the King.

Although the quantity of iron produced at this period must have been very small, yet our forefathers attained to great skill in working it with the hammer. We all know to what a state of perfection the manufacture of defensive armour was brought, and who can compare the beautiful specimens of mediæval iron work still to be found in and about our churches, with the coarse, cold, clumsy cast-iron ornaments of the present day? The former are both simple and effective, but the latter are essentially incapable of a fine line or shadow, and easily distinguishable from the wrought and hammered work of other days.

Up to the middle of the sixteenth century there were few improvements made in the slow and tedious method of iron-making; but, when at length those great and happy changes in the former political and social system took place, of which the Reformation was the cause, and an industrial and commercial spirit began to prevail, we find the iron trade assuming an importance in the country heretofore unknown; and to the early days of Elizabeth, or perhaps even to the reign of Edward VI., may be assigned the discovery of the blast furnace. The effect was soon felt in the country by the alarming decrease of timber, so that Acts of Parliament were passed " forbidding timber to be felled to make coals for burning iron," and the employment of timber trees of a given size was prohibited within certain districts ; but an exception was made for the county of Sussex, the Weald of Kent, and some parishes in Surrey, then great iron-making counties.  At the time of which we are speaking the iron trade was the staple manufacture of the county of Sussex, and there, in the parish of Buxted, in the year 1547, Peter Baud, a Frenchman, cast the first iron cannon ever so made in England.  Thomas Johnson, " covenant servant" to Peter, succeeded and exceeded his master, casting them cleaner and better.  He died about 1600.  Fuller, from whose book, *Worthies of England*, this notice of Sussex is taken, joins Evelyn in lamenting the decrease of timber ; but still, with faith and hope for the future, he adds— "It is to be hoped that a way may be found out to char sea coal in such manner as to render it useful for the making of iron.  All things are not found out in one age as reserved for future discovery, and that perchance may be easy for the next, which seems impossible to this generation."

Towards the close of the reign of Elizabeth blast furnaces had been erected of sufficient size to produce from two to three tons per day, or fifteen to twenty-one tons per week; such results, however, were only confined to works situated near an abundant stream of water, where water wheels of considerable magnitude could be used to work the bellows. The ironmasters now considered their own period as that of the highest pitch of advancement, and they looked with complacence and satisfaction upon the many improvements newly introduced.  The business seemed only limited to the supply of wood.  The scarcity soon became very serious. Petitions were presented and laws enacted against increas-

ing the number of ironworks. It soon became highly probable that many works must be shut up for ever, and the
trade in this country cease.

Under such unfavourable circumstances the discovery, or
rather the practicability, of making iron with pit coal, we
find announced by Simon Sturtevant, Esq., in the year 1612,
who obtained a patent for the exclusive manufacture of iron
with pit coal, for thirty-one years. The patentee did not
succeed, and the patent was surrendered. In 1613, John
Rovenson obtained a patent, who likewise failed, as did also
two other adventurers, by name Gambleton and Jordans.
In the year 1619, Dud Dudley, then a youth of 20 years of
age, was called home from Balliol College, Oxford, to manage
some iron works belonging to his father, Edward Lord
Dudley, in the chase of Pensnett, near Dudley; but wood
and charcoal becoming very scarce, and pit coal abounding,
he was induced to attempt to make iron with it. He was
successful, and a patent was granted him by King James.
Dud Dudley had great hardships and difficulties to contend
with. Rival manufacturers sought to deprive him of the
benefit of his invention—riotous persons cut the bellows
which blew his furnace—a great flood swept away his works
one May Day—his property was confiscated because of his
undeviating allegiance to the Crown during Cromwell's
tyrannical usurpation, and being imprisoned on occasion of
law suits and losses, he was compelled to desist from the
prosecution of his invention, although he tells us he had
been able to make iron "more sufficient, more cheap, and
more excellent." Dud Dudley lived to a good old age, and
now lies buried in the Church of S. Helen, Worcester,
where a monument was erected in memory of himself and
wife A.D. 1672.

The next attempt to make iron with pit coal was at Wednesbury. Mr. Blewstone, a German, so contrived a furnace that only the flame of the coal fire should come to the ironstone, but nevertheless it failed, although many were of opinion that he would succeed. The following is the reason given for this plan not answering :—" The sulphureous, vitriolic steams that issue from the pyrites, which frequently, if not always, accompanies pit coal, ascending with the flame poisoned the ore."

This account of Mr. Blewstone's attempt to make iron with pit coal, at Wednesbury, is taken from Dr. Plot's *History of Staffordshire*, as well as the following interesting particulars relating to the manufacture of iron in 1686 :—

" Iron ore they have from Wednesbury and Darlaston, but chiefly from Rushall. They have also some from Walsall, but not so good. Of the iron made of these they make the best wares, either mediately or immediately, the best iron of all being made out of the filings and pareings of the locksmiths, which they make up into balls with water, and dry them by the fire into hard balls ; then they put it into the fire and melt it by blast, licking it up with a rod of iron as they do glass at the glass-houses, and then beat it into a bar, which they use chiefly for keys and other fine works.

" When they have gotten the ore, before it is fit for the furnace, they burn or calcine it upon the open ground with small charcoal, wood, or sea coal, to make it break into small pieces, which will be done in three days, and this they call annealing it, or fitting it for the furnace. In the meanwhile they also heat their furnace for a week's time with charcoal without blowing it, which they call seasoning it, and then they bring the ore to the furnace thus prepared and throw it in with charcoal in baskets, alternately, namely, a

basket of ore, and then a basket of charcoal, where by two
vast pair of bellows placed behind the furnace, and compressed alternately by a large wheel turned by water, the fire
is made so intense, that after three days' time the metal will
begin to run, still after increasing, till at length in fourteen
nights' time they can run a sow and pigs once in twelve
hours, which they do in a bed of sand before the mouth of
the furnace, wherein they make one larger furrow than the
rest next the timp (where the metal comes forth), which is
for the sow, from whence they draw two or three-and-twenty
others (like the labels of a file in heraldry) for the pigs, all
which, too, they make greater or lesser according to the
quantity of their metal; into these when their receivers are
full they let it forth, which is made so very fluid by the
violence of the fire, that it not only runs to the utmost
distance of the furrows, but stands boiling in them for a considerable time. Before it is cold, that is, when it begins to
blacken at top, and the red to go off, they break the sow and
pigs off from one another, and the sow into the same length
with the pigs, though in the running it is longer and bigger
much, which is now done with ease; whereas if let alone
till they are quite cold, they will either not break at all, or
not without difficulty.

" In melting of iron ore some have great regard to the
make of the furnace and placing of the bellows, which that
the reader may the better apprehend, he must be informed
that the hearth of the furnace, into which the ore and coal
fall, is ordinarily built square, the sides descending obliquely
and drawing near to one another toward the bottom, like
the hopper of a mill. Where these oblique walls terminate,
which they term the boshes, there are joined four other
stones, but these are set perpendicular and reach to the

bottom stone, making the perpendicular square that receives
the metal, which four walls have the following names :—
that next the bellows, the tuarn or tuiron wall; that against
it, the wind wall or spirit plate ; that where the metal comes
forth, the timp or fore plate; that over against it, the back
wall; and these, according as they may be pitched, less
transhaw or more barrow, will mend, they say, or alter the
nature of the iron; if transhaw or transiring from the blast,
the iron will be more coldshear, less fined, more indeed to
the master's profit, but less to him that hath the manufac-
torage of it, and to him that useth it; whereas the iron
made in a barrow work is much more tough and serviceable.
Nor is the ordering of the bellows of less concern, which
have usually their entrance into the furnace between the
bottom of the hopper or boshes and the bottom stone,
and are placed nearer or further off, according as the ore
and metal require. 'Tis also of importance in melting of
iron ore that there be five or six soughs made under the
furnace, in parallel lines to the stream that turns the wheel,
which compresses the bellows to drain away the moisture
from the furnace, for should the least drop of water come
into the metal it would blow up the furnace, and the metal
would fly about the workmen's ears.

" From the furnaces they bring their sows and pigs of iron,
when broken asunder and into lengths, to the forges, which
are of two sorts, but commonly standing together under the
same roof; one whereof they call the finery, the other the
chafery; they are both of them open hearths, upon which
they place great heaps of coal, which are blown by bellows
like to those of the furnaces, and compressed the same way,
but nothing near so large.  In these two forges they give
the sow and pigs five several heats before they are perfectly

wrought into bars. First, in the finery, they are melted
down as thin as lead, where the metal in an hour thickens
by degrees into a lump or mass, which they call a loop,
this they bring to the great hammer, raised by the motion
of a water wheel, and, first, beat into a thick square, which
they call a half bloom; then, secondly, they put it into the
finery again for an hour, and then bring it again to the same
hammer, where they work it into a bloom, which is a square
bar in the middle, and two square knobs at the ends, one
much less than the other, the smaller being called the
ancony end, and the greater the mocket head. And this
is all they do at the finery. Then, thirdly, the ancony
end is brought to the chafery, where, after it has been
heated for a quarter of an hour, it is also brought to the
hammer, and there beat quite out to a bar, first at that end;
and after that the mocket head is brought, fourthly, to the
chafery, which, being thick, requires two heats, before it can
be wrought under the hammer into bars of such sizes and
shapes as they think fittest for sale.

" Whereof, those they intend to be cut into rods, are carried
to the slitting mills, where they first break or cut them,
cold, with the force of one of the wheels, into short lengths;
then they are put into a furnace to be heated red hot to a
good height, and then brought singly to the rollers, by which
they are drawn even, and to a greater length; after this
the workman takes them, whilst hot, and pushes them
through the cutters, which are of divers sizes, and may be
put off and on according to pleasure; then another lays
them straight, also whilst hot, and when cold binds them
into faggots, and then they are fitting for sale. And thus I
have given an account of the ironworks of Staffordshire,

Q

from the ore to the slitting mills, as they are now exercised in their perfection."

The following is the account given by S. T. Coleridge, Esq., of the introduction of slitting mills into this country. The descendants of the person who first brought them into use here being so immediately connected with Wednesbury, the anecdote will not be out of place.   It is as follows :—
"The most extraordinary and the best attested instance of enthusiasm existing, in conjunction with perseverance, is related of the founder of the Foley family.   This man, who was a fiddler, living near Stourbridge, was often witness of the immense labour and loss of time caused by dividing the bars of iron, necessary in the process of making nail rods, The discovery of the process of slitting was first made in Sweden, and the consequences of this advance in art were most disastrous to the manufacturers of iron about Stour-bridge.   Foley, the fiddler, was shortly missed from his accustomed rounds, and was not again seen for many years. He had mentally resolved to ascertain by what means the process of rod slitting was accomplished ; and, without communicating his intention to a single human being, he proceeded to Hull, and thence, without funds, worked his passage to the Swedish iron port.   Arrived in Sweden, he begged and fiddled his way to the ironworks, where, after a long time, he became a favourite with all the workmen ; and from the apparent entire absence of intelligence, or anything like ultimate object, he was received into the works, to every part of which he had free access.   He took the advantage thus offered, and, having stored his mind with observations and all the combinations, he disappeared from amongst his kind friends as he had appeared, no one knew whence or

whither. On his return to England, he communicated his voyage and its results to Mr. Knight and another person in the neighbourhood, with whom he was associated, and by whom the necessary buildings were erected and machinery prepared. When at length every thing was prepared, it was found that the machinery would not act; at all events it did not answer the sole end of its erection, viz., slitting bars into rods. Foley disappeared again, and it was concluded that shame and mortification at his failure had driven him away for ever. Not so; again, though somewhat more speedily, he found his way to the Swedish iron work, where he was received most joyfully, and to make sure of their fiddler he was lodged in the rod mill itself. Here was the very end and aim of his life attained beyond his utmost hope. He examined the works and very soon discovered the cause of his failure. He now made drawings, or rude tracings; and having abided an ample time to verify his observations, and to impress them clearly and vividly upon his mind, he made his way to the port, and once more returned to England. This time he was completely successful, and, by the results of his experience, enriched himself, and greatly benefited his countrymen." Another member of this family had the Iron Wire Works near Tintern Abbey, and other works at Whitbrook. Sir John Pettus tells us that this Mr. Foley employed at least 4,000 men daily at these and other iron works; and it is supposed that the entire number of persons employed in England in and about iron works, at the close of the 17th century, was upwards of 100,000.

The capabilities of this country for producing iron, provided some other fuel, instead of wood, could be introduced, seemed unbounded; but how to apply the only remedy, viz., pit coal, to the smelting of the iron ore, was the question. To this end a more powerful blast was necessary—one stronger than the bellows moved by a water-wheel could supply; and slowly, and by degrees, this was also being developed. The Marquis of Worcester, in 1663, had noticed and written upon the power of steam. Only one original copy of the interesting book in which his lordship recorded his various experiments is known to be in existence, and that is in the British Museum. Upon Lord Worcester's primitive attempt, Captain Savary, in 1698, made some improvements, and applied the power of steam to the draining of mines.* But to the great and comprehensive genius of the late Mr. Watt, we are indebted for those improvements, which have rendered the steam engine the present powerful agent of our ironworks, and herein he was assisted by the late Mr. Wilkinson, who, indeed, was the first, in Staffordshire, to apply the steam engine to blow the blast furnace, at the old furnace, near the Fire Holes, Bilston.

The regular and increased efforts of the blast furnace were soon felt in all the ironmaking districts, and the produce of the furnaces greatly increased. In 1740, just before the time of which we are now speaking, the total annual quantity of iron produced in Great Britian was 17,350 tons, whereas about the year 1608† the quantity was 180,000 tons, thus showing a very great falling off. In 1788, the total annual make was 68,300 tons, being an increase of 50,950 tons; whereas in 1796, the annual quantity exceeded 124,000 tons, which in 1820 was computed to be 400,000 tons; and in 1827, 690,000 tons. In the year 1846, the make had reached 1,750,000 tons; in 1851, 2,500,000

* See page 104, et seq.          † Sturtevant's Metallica.

tons; and the estimate for 1852 is 2,750,000 tons; whilst the number of hands, including colliers and miners, engaged in the iron business, is about 650,000.

In the year 1740, Gloucestershire produced a much greater quantity of iron than any other county in Britain, whilst Sussex contained the greatest number of furnaces. With a few in Kent, the residue required to make up the annual complement of iron were scattered sparingly throughout the midland counties and along the Welsh borders. Forty-eight years afterwards we find the coal counties begin to assume that rank in connection with iron, which for ages had been more particularly acceded to the woodland districts, and then it was that Staffordshire and Shropshire began to make those rapid strides towards importance as ironmaking counties that they have ever since maintained.

Many improvements have been made of late years in the various processes of the manufacture of iron. To Mr. Cort the country is indebted for the invention of puddling the pig iron, and rolling bars, in 1785; and, in 1829, to Mr. Neilson, of Glasgow, for the invaluable process of heating the blast previous to its entering the furnace. This produced a revolution next in importance to the application of the blast engine, for by it the weekly quantity made was increased from 80 or 90 tons to 120, 30, 40, 50, 60, and even in some instances to 200 tons per week. Scotland is greatly indebted to this discovery, for to it is mainly owing the development of the iron trade there. There is also another important feature connected with hot blast that must not be overlooked, which is this—that owing to its application furnaces worked better, both as to yield.

and quantity, and to so great an extent that it was deemed *practicable*, and proved since to be *advantageous, to stop them working on the Sabbath;* and there is no doubt that blast furnaces have made much more iron with standing on the Sunday than they used to do when working on that day, the *rationale* of which apparent paradox must be obvious to every mind. The late excellent Bishop of Lichfield, Dr. Ryder, addressed a letter of remonstrance to the ironmasters of his diocese on this subject, and some, acting upon his spiritual counsel, endeavoured to comply with his request; but the stopping of the furnaces on the Lord's Day was then found to be impracticable, as hot blast was not used. With all these great improvements and discoveries the iron trade has become one of the greatest manufacturing interests of the country, and it is now as it were the main spring, from which motion is given to our other improvements in steam engines, railroads, and machinery of all sorts.

# CHAPTER VII.

## Pottery.

——

The art of manufacturing earthenware vessels appears to have been known at a very early date, as is proved by the specimens of late years discovered in Egypt, Pompeii, Etruria, and Assyria; and that the ancient Britons were also acquainted with it is evidenced by the various remains found in their burial places. Some were rudely wrought, others more neatly fashioned, and many burnt in a kiln or furnace.

In all probability the art was imported by the first colonists of the country, and the Britons gradually improved the manufacture of it afterwards. The Roman invasion served to introduce many improvements, whereby the inhabitants would learn to model their vessels with a lathe, to give them the polish of a glazery, flourish them with carvings, and to emboss them with figures. This country occupies a prominent position in the history of the manufacture, from the ingenious discovery of Mr. Wedgwood, by which his pottery in Staffordshire was extended to a variety of curious compositions, subservient not only to the ordinary purposes of life, but to the arts, antiquity, history, &c., and thereby rendered a very important branch of commerce both foreign and domestic.

About the year 1650 there were several potteries in Wednesbury. The following account of them is transcribed from Dr. Plot :—" At Darlaston, near Wednesbury, there is tobacco pipe-clay found, but of late disused, because of better and cheaper found in Monway Field, between Wednesbury and Willingsworth, which is of a whitish colour, and makes excellent pipes. Besides this clay there is found in the same Monway Field two other sorts, one of a yellowish colour, mixed with white, the other bluish; the former stiff and weighty, the other more friable and light, which, mixed together, work better than apart; of these they make divers sorts of vessels at Wednesbury, which they paint with slip, made of a reddish earth, got at Tipton.* Also at Darlaston, near Wednesbury, is found a sort of blue clay, which is beaten up upon boards into oval cakes, and are sold to the glovers for about 4d. per dozen; these they use to give their wares an ash colour." The " slip" before mentioned is explained as " being clay of a more loose and friable nature, which, when mixed with water, is made into a consistence thinner than syrup, so that being put into a bucket it will run out through a quill, and with this they paint their wares. Before the clay is brought to the wheel, it is prepared by

* Some of these vessels were dug up in " Potter's Lane," at Wednesbury, in excavating for the South Staffordshire Railway.

steeping it in water in a square pit, till it be of a due consistence; then they bring it to the beating board, where it is beaten until well mixed; then being first made into great squarish rolls, it is brought to the weighing board, where it is slit into flat, thin pieces, with a wire, and all the stones picked out. Then they knead it like bread, and make it into round balls, and then bring it to the wheel and form it as the workman sees good. When the potter has wrought the clay, in fine weather he sets the vessels out to dry; but in foul, by the fire, and when dry they 'stoak' them (*i. e.* put ears and handles to them). These also being dry they paint them with the 'slip.' After the vessels are painted they 'lead' them with lead-ore, beaten into dust, finely sifted, and strewed upon them, which gives them the gloss, but not the colour. After this they are carried to the oven, which is ordinarily above eight feet high, and about six feet wide, of a round form, where they are placed upon one another. If they be wares not leaded, they are exposed to the naked fire; but if they be leaded ware, they do not expose them to the fire, but put them in coarse metallic pots, made of marl (not clay). In twenty-four hours an oven of pots will be burnt; then they let the fire go out by degrees, which takes ten hours more, and then they draw them for sale, which is chiefly to the poor cratemen, who carry them at their backs all over the country, to whom they reckon them by the piece, *i. e.*, quart in hollow ware, so that six pottle, or three gallon bottles make a dozen, and so more or less to the dozen, as they are of greater or less content. The flat wares are reckoned by pieces and dozens, according to their different breadths. With the clay about Wednesbury, also, they make a sort of arched bricks, bent round to fit the eyes

R

of their coal-pits, which are generally about two yards in diameter, by which they are secured from colting in, much better than by timbers, as I saw some pits, near that town, thus walled up with them for two yards deep, there being no necessity of doing it lower there, the clay being often stiff enough to uphold itself."

This trade, once so flourishing in Wednesbury, has now become extinct (unless we except the tobacco pipemaking), and the last potter removed from the parish about fifty years ago, and went to reside in the Staffordshire Potteries.

## CHAPTER VIII.

## Remarkable Characters and Incidents.

**A**lthough the town of Wednesbury can add but few names to the list of those who have distinguished themselves either in Church or State, yet it is said to have given rise to the noble family of Paget, whose present representative is the Marquis of Anglesea. The present Marquis has gained an illustrious name in being an energetic and brave defender of the liberties of Englishmen. The renown thus gained sheds a lustre upon Wednesbury, inasmuch as it is reported to have been the birth-place of his ancestor, William Lord Paget, who first saw the light amid the lowly cottages of the poor in this place, affording another example of what intelligence and honesty can effect. Although of humble origin, yet he became a distinguished politician in the reigns of Henry VIII., Edward VI., and Mary. He so recommended himself to Henry VIII., that he bequeathed to him by will £300, appointed him one of his executors, and of the council to his son Edward VI., in whose reign he was knighted, made Comptroller of the Household, Chancellor of the Duchy of Lancaster, and, in the year 1550, Lord Paget of Beaudesert, which manor, formerly belonging to the see of Lichfield, was made over to him.   He was at first in favour of the Reformed religion, but in his latter days became a rigid Papist.

The family of Parkes also deserves particular mention. They, likewise, were of obscure parentage, their ancestors having been nailers in or near Wednesbury.   In the year 1600, Willingsworth and the manor of Sedgley belonged to Thomas Parkes, who purchased it of Lord Dudley; and, by the marriage of his great granddaughter and sole heiress, Anne, with William, son of Humble Lord Ward, it was carried into that family.   Richard Jevon, of Sedgley, in 1608, exchanged with Thomas Parkes, of Willingsworth, five-sevenths of the tithes and rectory of Wednesbury (being himself one of the seven co-heirs to William Orme, gent., in the said tithes) for more lands in Sedgley.   The name of Parkes occurs frequently amongst the list of benefactors to the church and poor of Wednesbury; but this has been noticed in its proper place, as also their monuments in the chancel.   In the first year of Charles I., Thomas Parkes was High Sheriff of the county of Stafford.

The following is a copy of the original grant of arms to this family :—

**To all and singular,** as well nobles and gentlemen as others, to whome these presents shall come, I, Richard St. George, Esq., Norroy King of Arms of yᵉ north parts of yᵉ realm of England, greeting, forasmuch as it hath always been a rule in all well governed Commonwealths very requisite to grace and give credit to the virtuous and well deserving, as well for yᵉ encouragement of others to follow their steps in all honourable actions and heroical virtues, as also to distinguish the base and unworthy from men of good repute, by appropriating unto themselves and their descendants some sign or mark of honour, commonly called arms, and because the just reward of virtue is honour, and to detain a dutye where there were cause to yield it were injustice. Being, therefore, required by Richard Parkes, of Willingsworth, in yᵉ cᵒ· of Stafford, to rank him in yᵉ society of men of worth, as also finding him to be a man of such desert as he well deserveth to be accompted in yᵉ number, the premises, therefore, considered, I have thought fitt to confirm unto him these arms ensueing, videlt :—Sable a fess Ermine, between three bucks' heads, couped or. And for his crest on a wreath on his coullors—or and sable, an oak tree flourishing with leaves and acorns thereon, a squirrell all proper. I, the sᵈ· Norroy, doe grant, ratify, and confirm unto yᵉ sᵈ· Richard and his descendants, etc.—In witness, etc., etc.—Dated February 4, Anno 12, Jacobi (1615).—*Harl, MSS.*, 1052.

The family of Hopkins, also mentioned in the list of benefactors, resided at Oakeswell Hall, in Wednesbury, now the property of John Crowther, Esq. William Hopkins was a staunch supporter of Church and State. In the time of the Great Rebellion he suffered for his loyalty, as will be seen from the following :—

*Royalist Composition Papers in Her Majesty's State Paper Office. Second series, vol.* 27, *p.* 285.—*27th February,* 1646-7.

These are to certifie that William Hopkins, of Wednesbury, in the county of Stafford, gent., did freely and fully take the Nationall Covenant and subscribe the same upon the seven-and-twentieth day of Ffebruary, 1646 : the said Covenant being administered unto him according to order by mee.

(Signed)                 WILLM. BARTON,
                Minister of John Zacharies, London.

Probatus est ut notus.

*27th February,* 1646-7.—Mr. William Hopkins, within named, tooke the Negative Oath this 27th of Ffebruary, 1646.

(Signed)                 THOMAS VINCENT.

*Royalist Composition Papers in Her Majesty's State Paper Office. Second series, vol. 27, p. 284.—March 6, 1646-7.*

To the Honourable the Comittee at Goldsmith's Hall for com-pounding w^th. Delinquents,—

*The humble Petition of William Hopkins, of Wednesbury, in the County of Stafford,—*

Sheweth,—

That yo^r. petitioner did adhere & assist the Kinge ag^t. the Parliam^t. but finding his error did surrender and submitt himselfe to the Comittee of Stafford, in May, 1644, and hath taken the Nationall Covennt & Negative Oath, and hath been obedient to all ordinances of Parliam^t. & paid all taxes and assessm^ts. and ffree quarter.

Yo^r. petitioner, therefore, humbly prayeth this hono^ble. Comittee to admitt him to a favorable composicon for his delinquency to free his estate from sequestracon.

And he shall daily pray, &c.

(Signed)    WILLM. HOPKINS.

Rec^d. March 6, 1646, & referred to the Sub-Comittee.—(Signed) Jo. Leech.

---

*Royalist Composition Papers in Her Majesty's State Paper Office. Second series, vol. 27, p. 281.*

This is a true particular of all my estate, for w^ch. I desire to compound.

| | |
|---|---:|
| *In primis.*—That I am seized in ffee to me and my heirs of lands in Wednesbury, in the county of Stafford, yearly worth, before these troubles | 40 00 00 |
| That I am seized of a like estate of lands in Tipton, in the said county, yearly worth, before these troubles | 09 00 00 |
| That I am seized of a like estate of lands in West-bromw^ch. yearly worth, before these troubles | 10 00 00 |
| That I am seized of a like estate of one ten^t. in Walsall, in the said county, of the yearly value, before these troubles | 02 00 00 |
| That I am seized of a like estate of a parcell of meadowe in Broadesley, in the county of War-wicke, yearly worth, before these troubles | 02 00 00 |

That I am seized of a copyhold estate in Wednesbury aforesaid, to me and my heirs worth, before
these troubles, per an. .     .     .     . 06 00 00
I crave to be allowed for chief rents, paid to the
Lord of the Manor of Wednesbury for the premises  03 17 06
This is a true particular of all my estate, for which I desire to compound, and doe promise to pay such ffine as this honble. Committtee
shall impose upon me, in order to ffree my selfe and my estate from
sequestracon.

                    (Signed)          WILLM. HOPKINS.

-----

*Royalist Composition Papers in Her Majesty's State Paper Office.     Second
series, vol. 27, p. 289.*

*Staff. Ss.*—These are to certifie whom it may concerne, att the request
of William Hopkins, of Wednesburie, in the county of Staff. that the
lands and tenem^ts. of the said William Hopkins, w^th. in the severall limitts
and parishes hereunder menconed are assessed and taxed, and for many
yeares last paste, before the late warre, have bine assessed and taxed to
the Church and Poor, as hereafter followeth, viz. :—

*Staff.*                                    PER ANN.
Lands in Wednesburie, att     .     .     . 46 00 00
(Signed) WILLIAM HAWKES, Constable.
        GEORGE MEDDEWE, } Overseers for the
        THOMAS COOPER,   }     Poor.
Lands in Tipton     .     .     .     . 9 00 00
(Signed) WILLIAM KEELING, Constable.
        HENRY DUDLYE,    } Overseers for the
        WILLM. NICKLINE, }     Poor.
Lands in West Bromwich     .     .     . 10 00 00
(Signed) THOMAS JESSON, Constable.
        JOHN WAWDE,      } Overseers for the
        WALTER STEVENS,  }     Poor.
In Walsall—1 house     .     .     .     . 2 00 00
*Warr.*
In Bordesley, in Com. Warr.     .     . 2 00 00
                                        ———————
                                        69 00 00
                                        ———————

*Royalist Composition Papers in Her Majesty's State Paper Office. Second series, vol. 27, p. 287.—March 24, 1646-7.*

These are to certifie all whom it may concerne, that William Hopkins, of Wednesbury, in the county of Stafford, at the surrender of Rushall, upon the 22nd of May, 1644, was there, amongst other prisoners, at w<sup>ch.</sup> time, having for good reasons prevailed for my protection, he went unto his house at Wednesbury, where hee lived ever since, obedient to all orders and ordinances of Parliament, as I have been credibly informed by a certificat given to him by Captain Robert Tuthill, then Governor there.

Holdenby, the 24th of March, 1646.

(Signed)    B. DENBIGH.

---

*Royalist Composition Papers in Her Majesty's State Paper Office.— Second series, vol. 27, p. 287—27th March, 1647.*

WILLIAM HOPKINS, OF WEDNESBURY, IN THE COUNTY OF STAFFORD, GENT.

*His Delinquency.*—He did adhere and assiste the Kinge against y<sup>e</sup> Parliam<sup>t</sup> but he did render himselfe to the Parliam<sup>t</sup> 22d May, 1644, as by the Earle of Denbighe's certificate appeares.

He peticoned heere 6° Marcii, 1646.

He took the Naconall Covenant, 27° ffeb<sup>r</sup> 1646, before William Barton, Minister of John Zacharies, and the negative oath here the same day.

He compounds upon a perticuler delivered in under his hand, by which he doth submitt to such ffyne, &c. and by which it appeares

He is seized in ffee of lands in Wednesbury afores<sup>d</sup> of the yearly valew before these trobles, 40℔.

He is seised in ffee of land in Tipton, in the said county, of the yearly valew before these trobles, 9℔.

He is seised in ffee of lands in West bromw<sup>ch</sup> in the said county, of the yearly valew before these trobles, 10℔.

He is seized in ffee of a tenem<sup>t</sup> in Walsall, in the said county, of the yearly valew before these trobles, 2℔.

He is seized in ffee of part of a meadow in Broadesley, in the said county, of the yearly valew before these trobles, 2℔.

He is seised in ffee of a coppihold in Wednesbury, of y<sup>e</sup> yearly valew before these trobles, 6℔.

He craves allowance ffor a quitt rent of 3℔. 17s. 6d. per ann. which hee saith hee payes to the Lord of the Manor of Wednesbury for his lands in Wednesbury.

(Signed)    WILL. THOMSON.

27 Marcii, 1647.

(Signed)   R. GURDON.

30 March, 1647.   Fine £195 10s. 6d.

———

*Royalist Composition Papers in Her Majesty's State Paper Office.—First series, vol. 113, p. 177.*

*Extracted from the Reports of the Committee for Compounding with Delinquents.*

WILLIAM HOPKINS, OF WEDNESBURY, IN THE COUNTY OF STAFFORD, GENT.

*His Delinquency.*—That he assisted the fforces raised against the Parliam*t.*

He render'd the 6th of March, 1646.

His estate in ffee per annum 69℔., ffor w*ch* his ffine, at a sixt, is 207℔.

———

*Royalist Composition Papers in Her Majesty's State Paper Office.—Second series, vol. 27, p. 291.*

STAFF. Ss.—BY THE COMITTEE.

These are to certifie all whom it may concerne, that WILLIAM HOPKINS, of Wednesbury, in this county, gent., having formerly borne armes ag*t* the Parliam*t* did, at or about the 24th of Aprill last past, when our fforces had beleaguered the Garrison of the Closse of Lichfield, submit himselfe to the Parliam*t* and did then compound w*th* this comittee for his personall estate, and his lands for the yeare then ensewing, and thereupon wee gave him a protection, and since he hath lived at his own house and carried himselfe inoffensively to the Parliam*t* for ought wee knowe.

Dated at Stafford, this 17th of March, 1646.

(Signed)        E. MAINWARING,
                LEICESTER BARBOUR,
                HEN. STONE,
                PHIL. JACKSON.

S

The Comberford family, of Comberford, near Tamworth, after inheriting the manor, resided in Wednesbury. The following superstition connected with this family is recorded by Dr. Plot :—" Besides extreme old age, we must not forget to reckon amongst the forerunners of death those signal warnings which some families have before the approaches of it  .  .  .  .  such is the knocks before the death of any of the family of the Comberfords, three knocks being always heard at Comberford Hall before the decease of any of that family, though the party dying be at never so great a distance." Henry Comberford, D.D., was made Precentor of Lichfield Cathedral, December 19, 1555; and, in 1559, he was deprived of all his benefices on account of his religion, and ordered to remain in Suffolk, at a great distance from his friends. In 1579 he was a prisoner, at the age of 80, at Hull, for his religious opinions were dangerous to the State. Lord Shrewsbury, writing to Lord Burley, from Sheffield Castle, January 20, 1572, says, " I caused my man to apprehend one Thomas Comberford, of Comberford, gent. He was concerned in the conspiracies of Queen Mary against Queen Elizabeth."

Roger Wednesbury was reprimanded and punished for misdemeanor, at the visitation of Hales Owen Abbey, held by the Bishop of Worcester, May 5, 1481.

Roger Weddesbury was Prior of Worcester from 1507 to 1578.

At the herald's visitation of Staffordshire, in 1664, Josiah Freeman, of Wednesbury, was disclaimed, not being entitled to the arms he had adopted.

At the visitation of 1583, held at Wolverhampton, William Hoo, of Bradley, was also disclaimed.

In Pope Nicholas's taxation, A.D. 1291, Wednesbury was allotted to pay 12s. 4d.

*Record Office, Carlton Ride, London.*

*Vicesima Domino Regi a laicis concessa in Com^tu· Staffordie, anno regni sui primo, (i.e. 1st Edward III.,) 1327.*

### WEDNESBURY.

| | | |
|---|---|---|
| De Juliana de Hervile . | iiij^a· | iiij^d· q. |
| De Matilda de Grete | | xiij^d· ob. |
| De Rogero de Brynghul | ij^a· | iij^d· |
| De Ricardo de Erbury | | xxiij^d· |
| De Galfrido Henrys | iij^a· | ij^d· |
| De Johanne Attezate | iij^a· | ob. q. |
| De Henrico Atteliderate | iij^a· | ob. q. |
| De Hugone Aleyn . | ij^a· | ob. |
| De Johanne atte Grene . | | ij^d· ob. q. |
| De Johanne Dymmok | | viij^d· |
| De Johanne Hanrys | | x^d· |
| De Johanne de Hervile | | iij^d· q. |

The following is taken from the *Talbot Papers*, letter N., fo. 247, in the College of Arms, London, being the subsidies for Staffordshire, shewing the yearly value of every parish, and property of every householder in the said county, A.D. 1590 :—

### WEDDESBURY.

| | | |
|---|---|---|
| William Cumbford Ar in terr xiij^e· | xxxiiij^a· | viij^d· |
| Tho. Walsted in terr iij^e· | x^a· | viij^d· |
| George Hopkins in terr iij^e· | | viij^a· |
| Thomas Merihurste in terr iij^e· | | viij^a· |
| William Watson in terr xx^e· | ij^a· | viij^d· |
| Richard Jenninge in bon vij^e· | xj^a· | viij^d· |
| Nicus Tankes in terr iij^e· | | viij^a· |
| Tho. Parkes in bon vj^e· | | x^a· |
| Ric. Sheldon in bon vj^e· | | x^a· |

George Meadowe in bon iij    .    .    v<sup>s.</sup>
Henry Sydowe in bon iij<sup>s.</sup>    .    .    .    v<sup>s.</sup>
Raphe Tonkes in bon iij<sup>s.</sup>    .    .    .    v<sup>s.</sup>
William Sedowne in bon iij<sup>s.</sup>    .    .    .    v<sup>s.</sup>
John More, sen. in bon iij<sup>s.</sup>    .    .    .    v<sup>s.</sup>
George Jesson in bon iij<sup>s.</sup>    .    .    .    v<sup>s.</sup>
Thomas Hopkins in bon iij<sup>s.</sup>    .    .    v<sup>s.</sup>

Sm<sup>a.</sup> vj<sup>s.</sup> xviij<sup>s.</sup> viij<sup>d.</sup>

Bordesley Monastery, in Worcestershire, possessed a water mill in Wednesbury, valued at 28s. yearly.

Sandwell Monastery also held lands in Wednesbury.

Thomas Knight founded a charity in Walsall church, and endowed it with lands in Wednesbury. It was valued at £4 6s. 1d.

April 8, 1643, it was ordered that the weekly pay of Willenhall, Wednesbury, &c., should be assigned to Colonel Leigh, of the rebel army, to pay his company and officers; and, June 22, 1644, it was again ordered that the weekly pay of Walsall, West Bromwich, Sandwell, Tipton, and Wednesbury, should be assigned to Captain Tuttle, of the Parliamentary army, for the pay of his officers and soldiers.

The Treasurer of the King's Garrison at Lichfield received from the constablewick of Wednesbury, in October, November, and December, 1645, five pounds for the royal cause.

William Hopkins, yeoman, and Richard Hawkes and Robert Carter, caused the chimes of the Parish Church to be made and set up at their equal and proper cost and charges, A.D. 1635.

The following curious extracts are made from the Parish Registers, and are here inserted as likely to prove interesting to some :—

1673.—Elizabeth Dutton was buried, being about 100 years old.

1674.—John Russell being famished for want of bread, (Josiah Freeman being overseer,) with the solemnity of many tears was buried.

1677.—John Beck, an ancient widower and true Churchman, was buried.

1678.  Elizabeth Webb, an ancient widow, being 100 years of age, was buried.

After the act passed in the year 1678, entitled "An Act for burying in Woollen," the registers certify when it was adhered to, and the first affidavit was made before Captain Thomas Lane, eldest son of the famous Colonel Lane, of Bentley, who afforded protection to the fugitive monarch, Charles II.

1687.—A child of Robert Beardsmore, a most rude, swearing collier, was buried in woollen only.

1701.—Thomas Robinson, a Quaker, of the parish of Darlaston, was put into a pit, that was made in the yard adjoining the Quakers' Meeting House, in the Parish of Wednesbury.  Of this no affidavit was given that the body was wrapped in woollen, and the curate gave notice thereof to the churchwardens, as the act required, to avoid the penalty.

1701.—John, the son of George and Mary Newall, Roman Catholicks, was born at the Delves, and baptized, as I was informed, by a person of the Romish persuasion.

This is the first evidence of Romanism existing in Wednesbury after the Reformation.

1702.—John, the son of John and Elizabeth Cashmore, was baptized by a Presbyterian minister, at St. Margaret's Chapel *alias* a barn, in the parish of West Bromwich.

1703.—Martha, the daughter of Edward and Martha Heywood, was baptized by a Presbyterian minister, at a conventicle, at the house of William Clare, of Tipton, an old Oliverian cornet.

The names which occur most frequently in ancient registers are the following (some of which are to be met with at the present day):—"Addenbrooke, Babb, Bruisbones, Bassett, Biram, Collier, Cheshire, Dearlove, Danks, Darlaston, Jesson, Hawke, Hopkins, Hurlbut, Holden, Merryhurst, Meadow, Parkes, Parkshouse, Pershouse, Palmer, Richards, Ratliffe, Siddons, Spittle, and Tonks."

The trades formerly followed, as shown by the same authority, were those of " nailmakers, forgemen, colliers, tobacco-pipe-makers, bucklemakers, potters, gun-lock-makers, curtain-ring-makers (at the Delves,) brickmakers, boremakers, vicemakers, weavers, dyers, hatters, bendwaremakers, tow-dressers, and edge-tool-makers."

The places most frequently mentioned are " the Delves, King's Hill, Monway Field, (these two names occur in a document A.D. 1315,) the Pits, Wednesbury Mill, the Forge, the Bridge End, and Broadwaters;" this latter place, Dr. Plot tells us, " was stocked at the first with fish by Mr. Lane, of Bentley." The same author relates the following circumstance :—" Of all the accidents that can befall the trunks of trees, there is none more unaccountable than their being found in divers countries buried under ground; . . . . they are found in Rotten Meadow, under Wednesbury Hall, and also near Wrottesley," &c. &c.

" Of unusual small birds I would add," says Dr. Plot, " the Fringilla Montana, or mountain chaffinch, of the short, hard-beaked kind, found plentifully about Venice, but rarely in England. This I have was killed and given me by the ingenious Mr. Millar, Vicar of Wednesbury, near the Vicarage House."

In writing of the eggs of birds, the Doctor states :—
"Herein I also met with divers anomalies of Nature.  The
ingenious Mr. Millar, Vicar of Wednesbury, amongst his
tithe-eggs, met with one whose yolk was perfectly white as
that we usually call so, the separation between them remaining as distinct as in ordinary eggs."

Of meteors he writes :—" A meteor of a globular form
was seen November 22nd, 1672, about twelve or one at
night, not in motion, but stationary, against the west door
of Wednesbury Church, by the ingenious Mr. Millar, Vicar
there, and two others in his company, which shone so bright
that it gave them light, though a very dark night, at half a
mile distance, where it continued for about the one-eighth
of an hour's space, and then of a sudden disappeared ;
whereupon there immediately followed a great storm of hail
and rain."

" We need go no further," says the Doctor, " for an
instance of unknown noises than in the same town of Wednesbury, where the colliers will tell you that, early in the
morning, as they go to their work, and from the colepits
themselves they sometimes hear the noise of a pack of
hounds in the air, which has happened so frequently, that
they have got a name for them, calling them ' Gabriel's
hounds,' though the more sober and judicious take them
only to be wild geese, making their noise in their flight,
which perhaps may be probable enough."

Speaking of echoes, the same writer observes :—"I was
informed by the ingenious Mr. Millar, Vicar of Wednesbury,
that there is a very distinct echo there, when the windmill
window stands open towards the church, otherwise none at

all, two of the three windmills there answering the five
bells orderly and distinctly."

Snelling, in his work on coins, published in 1723, mentions a "Wednesbury token."

The Rev. Edward Best, then vicar of the parish, mentions
in a letter to a friend, that in 1761 the smallpox raged
fearfully in Wednesbury.

# Appendix.

———

FOR the better and easier administration of justice, the country was divided, at a very early period, into counties, hundreds, and tithings, over each of which presided a magistrate; over the county, a count, earl, or alderman; over the hundred, a hundred man; over the tithing, a decanus or tithing man. Each of these officers held a court, in which justice was administered, and all affairs of the district discussed, and public matters carried on, such as sales and other transactions, in which publicity was requisite. These courts formed a graduated scale, and admitted of appeals from the lower to the higher court, so that from the decision of the tithing there lay an appeal to that of the hundred, and from that of the hundred to that of the *shire*. From this plan arose the system of "*frankpledge*," which was divided into two branches; the first being the seignoral or personal liability of the superior, which rendered him the permanent surety for the appearance of his vassal, retainer, or inmate; and, the second the collective or natural responsibility of the villainage, as included in their tithings, associations which, in the Saxon era, were of unequal extent, according to the custom of the country, *ten* being the *smallest* number of which a tithing could be composed, and from whence it derived its name.

T

APPENDIX B.—*Grant of Walsall Church, with its Chapels, by King Henry III. to Hales Owen Abbey, A.D. 1245.—Extracted from the " Registrum Album," in the custody of the Dean and Chapter of Lichfield, p. 243.*

Henricus Dei gracia Rex Anglie Dominus Hibernie Dux Normannie Aquitanie Comes Andegavie Archiepiscopis Episcopis Abbatibus Prioribus Comitibus Baronibus Justiciariis vice Comitibus Prepositis Ministris et omnibus ballivis et fidelibus suis salutem. Sciatis nos intuitu Dei et pro salute anime nostre et animabus antecessorum et heredum nostrorum dedisse concessisse et hac carta nostra confirmasse quantum ad patronum pertinet pro nobis et heredibus nostris Deo et Ecclesie Beate Marie de Hales et fratri Ricardo Abbati ejusdem loci et Canonico de ordine Premonstratensi ibidem Deo seriuentibus et successoribus suis ibidem Deo seruituris in perpetuum Ecclesiam de Waleshal cum omnibus Capellis ad eandem eccclesiam spectantibus et omnibus aliis pertinenciis suis, habendam et tenendam in liberam puram et perpetuam elemosinam. Quare volumus et firmiter precipimus pro nobis et heredibus nostris quod predicti Abbas et Canonici et successores sui habeant et teneant predictam eoclesiam de Waleshale cum omnibus Capellis libertatibus et aliis pertinenciis ad eandem ecclesiam spectantibus bene et in pace libere et quiete in liberam puram et perpetuam elemosinam sicut predictum est His testibus, Ricardo fratre nostro Comite Cornubye, Ricardo de Clare Comite Gloucestrie, Simone de Monte forti Comite Leycestrie, Humfrido de Boun Comite Herfordie, Petro de Saband, Willielmo de Eboraco preposito Beverlaci, ffulconi filio Warini, Paulino Pryner, Gilberto de Segrave, Johanne extraneo, Roberto Muscegros, Roberto le Norreys, Anketell Malvri, et aliis.—Datæ per manum nostram apud Wodestock, 15 die Julij. Anno regni nostri 29.

———

APPENDIX C.—*Extract from " Placita de Quo Warranto" (Record Publication), Edwd. I. (A.D. 1293), and the Abbot and Convent of Hales Owen, touching the right of presentation to the Church of Wednesbury, etc.*

DOMINUS REX per predictum Hugonem petet versus Abbatem de Hales Oweyn advocacionem ecclesiæ de Waleshale ut jus, &c. Et versus eundem Abbatem advocacionem capelloe de Wednesbury ut jus etc. et unde dicit quod dominus Johannes Rex fuit seisitus in dominico suo ut de feodo et jure tempore pacis etc, tempore ejusdem Johannis presentando ad easdem quosdam Willhelmum et Johannem clericos suos, &c. Et de ipso Johanne Rege descendit jus, &c. Et quod tale sit jus, &c. paratus est verificare pro Rege, &c.

Et Abbas venit et defendit jus suum quondam, &c. Et dicit quod dominus Rex Henricus pater domini Regis nunc dedit et concessit Deo et Beatoe Marioe de Hales et fratri Ricardo Abbati ejusdem loci predecessori predicti Abbatis ecclesiam de Waleshale cum omnibus capellis ad eandem spectantibus et omnibus aliis pertinentibus suis habendam in puram and perpetuam elemosinam per cartam ipsius Henrici Regis quam profert et quæ hoc idem testatur. Et dicit quod predicta capella de Wednesbury est pertinens ad predictam ecclesiam de Waleshale et fuit tempore concessionis predictæ, &c.

Et Hugo de Louther qui sequitur, &c. dicit predicto tempore quo dominus Henricus Rex predictus concessit predicto Abbati advocacionem illam cum capella predicta de Wednesbury non fuit de pertinentibus ecclesiæ predictæ de Waleshale. Et hoc paratus est verificare pro Rege, &c.

Et Abbas dicit quod tempore concessionis predictæ et semper postea predicta capella fuit pertinens ad predictam ecclesiam de Waleshale. Et de hoc ponit se super patriam. Et predictus Hugo similiter. Et Robertus de Hasteng, Adam de Brunton, Johannes filius Philippi, Johannes de Herumville, Thomas de Hamstede, Ricardus de Pyrye, Wilhelmus de Wrotteslegh, Philippus de Luttelee, Ricardus Geru, Warin de Penne, Robertus de la Blome de Tybyngton, and Thomas de Luttelegh, jurati de assensu ipsius Abbatis ad hoc electi dant super sacramentum suum quod predicta capella de Wednesbury, fuit matrix ecclesia ante donacionem et concessionem quas predictus Henricus Rex fecit predicto Abbati et successoribus suis de ecclesia de Waleshale cum capellis ad eandem pertinentibus et antequam predicta eccelsia de Waleshale fuisset matrix ecclesia et non capella pertinens ad predictam ecclesiam de Waleshale. Imo constitutus est quod dominus Rex recuperet seisam suam de advocacione predictæ capellæ de Wednesbury. Et Abbas in misericordia. Et mandatus est Coventrensi et Lichfeldensi Episcopo non obstante reclamacionem predicte Abbatis, &c. ad presentacionem domini Regis ad predictam capellam idoneam personam admittat, &c.

APPENDIX D.—*Grant of the right of presentation to the Church of Wednesbury to the Abbot and Convent of Hales Owen, by King Edward I.,
1301, also the Abbot's agreement to pay 10 marks to Nicholas de Burton,
(who had been appointed Vicar of Wednesbury by the King), in case he
would resign.—Extracted from the " Registrum Album," in the possession
of the Dean and Chapter of Lichfield, p. 244.*

Edwardus Dei gracia Rex Anglie Dominus Hibernie et Dux Aquitanie
Omnibus ad quos presentes litere pervenerint salutem.    Sciatis quod per
finem quem dilectus nobis in Christo Abbas de Hales Oweyn ordinis Premonstratensis, fecit nobiscum coram Thesaurario et Baronibus nostris de
Scaccario dedimus et concessimus pro nobis et heredibus nostris eidem
Abbati et Conventui ejusdem loci advocacionem capelle de Wedenesbury
cum pertinenciis Coventrie et Lichfeldie dioceseos quam dudum in Curia
nostra coram dilectis et fidelibus nostris Johanne de Berwyk et sociis suis
justiciariis nostris itinerantibus in Comitatu Staffordie per consideracionem
ejusdem Curie versus Nicholaum quondam Abbatem de Hales prede-
cessorem predicti Abbatis recuperavimus ut jus nostrum   Habendam et
tenendam eisdem Abbati et Conventui et successoribus suis de nobis et
heredibus nostris in liberam et puram elemosinam in perpetuum.   Et
insuper concessimus eis pro nobis et heredibus nostris quantum in nobis
est quod ipsi capellam predictam cum pertinenciis suis super usus proprios
perpetuo possidendam appropriare et eam sic appropriatam tenere possint
suis et successoribus suis sine occasione vel impedimento nostri vel heredum
nostrorum in perpetuum.   In cujus rei testimonium has literas nostras
fieri fecimus patentes.  Teste me ipso.  Kemeseye quinto die Maij anno
regni nostri vicesimo nono.—5 May, 1301.

Rotulus placetorum coram Domino Rege apud Wigorn de term Pasch.
Anno regni Regis Edwardi filius Regis Henrici xxixno. Gillbertus de
Ronbury Willhelmus de Ormseby Henricus Spigurnell tenentes locum
Domini Regis in absencia Rogeri de Brabanson.

Abbas de Hales Oweyn venit et recognovit quod concessit Nicholo
Burton cui Dominus Rex concessit advocacionem capellæ de Wednesbury quam ipse Dominus Rex recuperavit versus dictum Abbatem
coram justiciis itinerantibus & quam dictus Abbas dedit sibi pertinere
ut capellam ecclesiæ suæ de Waleshale & pro eo quod dominus Rex
nunc concessit dicto Abbati & successoribus suis dictam capellam ipse

Abbas concessit (Nicholaus?) dicto Nicholao quandam annuitatem x marcarum solvendam eo quod ipse resignavit dicto Abbati totum jus suum &c.

*Record Office, Tower of London.*

*Patent Roll, 21st Edward I., Membrane 21.*

Nicholaus de Burtone habet litteras Regis de presentacione ad capellam de Wednesbury vacantem et ad donacionem Regis spectantem et diriguntur littere Couentrie et Lichfeldie Episcopo. Teste Rege apud Gerndone iiij die Marcij.

APPENDIX E.—*Deed of the Bishop of Coventry and Lichfield, confirming the foregoing. A.D.* 1305—*Extracted from the " Registrum Album,"* in the custody of the Dean and Chapter of Lichfield, p. 244.

W. permissione divina Coventrie et Lichfeldie Episcopus dilectis filiis Abbati et Conventui de Hales Ordinis Premonstratensis Salutem.

Ad perpetuam memoriam subscriptorum licet personis et locis religiosis non indigne debeatur promptitudo favoris. Summa tamen religiosa honestas que in vestro monasterio precipue exercetur speciali, quodam favore meretur ut sicut bonorum operum exerciciis in splendore summe charitatis intestitis. Sicut est condignum vos ac vestrum monasterium studeamus attollere incrementis. Sane in antedicte charitatis memoria R. quondam Coventrie et Lichfeldie Episcopi predecessoris nostri . .

. . quas oculis nostris subjecimus contineri inspeximus. Quod idem Episcopus monasterii vestri bonorum exilitatem conspiciens, simulque paupertati vestre compaciens, ecclesiam de Wednesbury nostre Dioceseos Capitulorum suorum Coventrie et Lichfeldie, accedente consensu vestris ac successoribus vestrorum usibus propriis perpetuo applicandam pietatis intuitu vobis duxerat concedendam prout in scriptis prefati predecessoris nostri sigillo quo utebatur plenius continetur cumque ecclesiam ipsam de Wednesbury per longa subsequentia demissetis tempora vestris ac successorum vestrorum usibus taliter applicatis, Serenissimus Princeps Edwardus Dei gratia Rex Anglie inclitus intellecto quod jus patronatus ipsius ecclesie de Wednesbury, ad ipsam coronam et dignitatem suam ab antiquo spectasset patronatum memoratum in foro seculari in quo placita hujusmodi in regno ipso exerceri solent

a vobis et monasterio vestro per judicium fori sui . . . . . . . .
ab ea sie vos amovens et clerico seculari faciens assignari eandem verum
cum processu temporis per hoc vidissetis vos ac vestrum monasterium
graviter fore lesum ac irreparabili ruine in vicino inseparabiliter . . .
subjacendum vos Domini Regis vestris anyetatis et continuis clamoribus
intus compacientis tantam ministris graciam optinere quod idem Dominus
Rex in vos successoresque vestros ac monasterium vestrum jus patronatus
predicti in perpetuis transtulit temporibus intuitu pietatis iæ . . . .
ulterius contemplacione vestra facietis graciose quod clericus qui ex
donacione ipsius Regis ecclesiam ipsam tenuerat ob ejusdem domini
Regis reverenciam omnino dimisit eandem ad vos successoresque vestros
quantum in eis Domino Rege et clerico servato revertendam. Porro post
hæc omnia oculos lacrimarum vestrarum in nos continuatis instanciis
assidue convertentes nostre solicitudinis studium stimulari ac nobis
indefinenter clamando supplicare cessastis ut cum tam Regis quam
clerici benevolentiam in hac parte fueritis assecuti ad vos et monasterium vestrum de cujus ruina lamentabili verisimiliter timebatur pietatis
oculum prout ad nos pertinet extendere ac vos et monasterium vestrum
ad statum quem in ecclesia predicta antiquitus habebatur pietate paterna
reducere quin pocius mero gracie nostre ministerio ecclesiam ipsam
cum suis juribus vestris ac successorum vestrorum usibus propriis applicandam concedere dignaremur. Nos itaque vestre ac monasterii vestri
(paupertati notorie compacientes ac predecessoris nostri) R. felicis
recordacionis vestigiis inherentes consideracione et excellentissimi Prin-
ipis Domini nostri E. Regis Anglie illustris pro vobis in hac parte
assidua instancia supplicantis ecclesiam de Wednesbury memoratam cum
suis juribus et pertinenciis universis Capitulorum nostrorum Couentrie
et Lichfeldie accedente consensu vobis ac monasterio vestro in Dei
nomine cum perpetua devocione seruitis presencium tenore concedimus
vestris ac successorum vestrorum usibus propriis perpetuo applicandam.
Et ad perpetuam horum memoriam tam sigillum nostrum quam Coven_
trie et Lichfieldie capitulorum nostrorum sigilla presentibus sunt appensa
Data per nos Episcopum apud Brewode xviii. Kalendas Septembris et
per nos Priorem et Capitulum Couentrie in Capitulo nostro Couentrie xv.
Kalendas Septembris. Et per nos Decanum et Capitulum Lichfeldie in
Capitulo nostra Lichfeldie, xi Kalendas Septembris Anno Domini Mil-
lesimo CCC$^{mo.}$ quinto et consecracionis nostre prefati Episcopi anno nono.
—August 15, 18, 22, 1305.

APPENDIX F.—*Charter of Sir William Rous or Rufus concerning Walsall Church.*

Omnibus sanctæ matris ecclesiæ filiis, ad quas præsens scriptum pervenerit, Willielmus Rufus de Waleshale, salutem. Noverit universitas vestra, me causa Dei et intuitu pietatis dedisse, concessisse, et hac mea presenti carta confirmasse Deo et ecclesiæ S. Mariæ de Hales, et canonicis ordinis Premonstratensis ibidem Deo servientibus, ecclesiam de Waleshale cum capellis et pertinentiis, et omnibus aliis libertatibus suis ; habendam et possidendam in liberam puram et perpetuam eleemosynam, ad hospitalitatem ejusdem domus sustentandam, pro salute animæ meæ, et omnium antecessorum et successorum meorum. His testibus, domino P. Win.toniensi episcopo ; domino Willielmo Coventrie episcopo ; domino R. abbate de Wellebec, Henrico de Aldetheleg ; Roberto Marmiun ; Willielmo Marmiun fratre ejus ; Ricardo filio Willielmi de Brameurice ; Willielmo Hasato ; Ada de Sancta Maria ; Thoma capellano de Hales.

---

*Other Documents relating to Wednesbury, Rushall, and Walsall.—Extracted from the " Registrum Album," in the custody of the Dean and Chapter of Lichfield, p.* 243.

Universis Sancte Matris Ecclesie filiis ad quos presens scriptum pervenerit. Frater Rogerus permissione divina Prior Coventrie et ejusdem loci Conventus Salutem in Domino sempiternam. Noverit universitas vestra nos inspexisse ordinacionem venerabilis patris Rogeri Coventrie et Lichfeldie Episcopi et magistri Ricardi thesaurarii in hæc verba.

Universis Christi fidelibus ad quos presens scriptum pervenerit Rogerus Dei gracia Couentrie et Lichfeldie Episcopus et Ricardus thesaurarius Lichfeldie salutem in Domino sempiternam. Noverit Universitas vestra quod cum Henricus Dei gracia Rex Anglorum illustris Abbati et Conventui de Hales Premonstratensis ordinis quorum ecclesiam pater ejus fundaverat patronatum ecclesie de Waleshale contulisset optans quod ecclesie fructus in usus cederent eorundem iidem Abbas et Conventus ordinacioni nostre se supposuerunt quo ad ecclesiam antedictam et pertinencia ejus que in eorum literis patentibus super confectis plenius continetur. Nos igitur dicti Domini Regis affectum pium in domino commendantes desiderantesque perfectum dictorum Religiosorum quibus propter confluenciam hospitum ut dicitur prope non suppetunt ffacultates divine caritatis intuitu et ob ejusdem dicti domini Regis reuerenciam et ad ejus instanciam de consensu Capituli Lichfeldie ordinando decreuimus quod cum Magister Vincentius Rector Ecclesie de Waleshale ipse cesserit vel decesserit dicti Abbas et Conventus dictam ecclesiam de Waleshale habeant cum pertinenciis et fructibus ejus in usus proprios convertendo. Salva tunc vicaria xiv. marcis assignandis vicario per viros fideles et discretos ad hoc per episco pum deputatos in terris obvencionibus ecclesie quod et aream et edificia ecclesie dividant inter predictos religiosos et vicarium secundum quod racione prima viderunt expediri. Vicariusque qui pro tempore fuerit onera episcopalia et Archidiaconalia consueta et debita sustinebit ad onera vero Capellarum ecclesie de Walshale consueta scilicet de Wednesbury, et de Rushal et servicia sibi debita sustinenda habeat idem vicarius preter xii. marcas super fructum quod dictum est superius assignando omnes obuenciones Capellarum earundem propter garbas que quidem obuenciones si ad servicia ac onera in predictis Capellis in forma premissa sustinenda non sufficiant in aliis ejusdem ecclesie proventibus una cum eisdem obuen- cionibus per viros suprascriptos dicto vicario providentur unus in preno- minatis Capellis eadem servicia et onera honeste valeat sustinere alia vero onera Abbas et vicarius similiter pro suis porcionibus sustinebunt. Saluo eciam quod Abbas et Conventus supradicti singulis annis solvant Ecclesie Lichfeldie sex marcas pro ad peticionem dictorum Abbatis et Conventus duximus ordinando ad eorum perpetuam pacem super ecclesiam sepedictam in qua se dicebat aliquando Lichfeldie ecclesia jus habere. De dictis autem sex marcis sexaginta solidos deputamus ad sustentacionem operis Ecclesie Lichfeldie, residuos vero viginti solidos vicariis qui ad missam Beate Virginis vicissim per annum secundum quod moris est fuerint deputati per Capellanum Beate virginis ipsis dicta pecunia tribu- enda. Qui dicti viginti solidi solui debeant. Sexaginta vero solidi ipsi qui ad custodiam fabrice fuerit deputatus terminis infrascriptis. Ita scilicet quod tres marce solvantur apud Lichfeldiam in festo Sancti Michaelis tres vero residue in festo Resurrexionis dominice persoluantur. Jurabit et dictus Abbas de Hales qui pro tempore fuerit se dictas sex marcas dictis terminis fideliter soluturum. Non licebit a Decano et Capitulo Lichfeldie in aliquos usus quam supradictos converti pecuniam memoratam. In premissorum autem testimonium et munimen presentem paginam sigillis nostris et sigillo Decani et Capituli Lichfeldie et Abbatis et Conventus de Hales in consensus sui testimonium fecimus roborari. Saluo Conventrie et Lichfeldie ecclesie juribus pont et paroch. Data apud Lichfeldiam in Crastino beati Thome Martyris, Anno Domini Millesimo CC. quadragesimo octavo. Dec. 30, 1248.

Nos igitur predictam ordinacionem ratam habentes et gratam. Eam sicut juste et racionabiliter factam esse. Auctoritate Ecclesiæ nostre Cathedrali confirmamus et huic scripto sigillum nostrum apposuimus in testimonium. Acta die Sabbati proxime post Purificacionem Beate Virginis. Anno. supradicto. February 6, 1248-9.

---

*Extracted from the "Registrum Album," in the custody of the Dean and Chapter of Lichfield, p. 245.*

Universis sancte matris ecclesie filiis ad quos presens scriptum pervenerit Rogerus Miseracione divina Coventrie et Lichfeldie Episcopus salutem in Domino sempiternam. Noveritis nos ordinacionem bone memorie Roger de Weseham Coventrie et Lichfeldie Episcopi predecessoris nostri super ecclesia de Waleshale, cum suis Capellis, videlicet de Wednesbury de Rushale, ac ceteris omnibus ad eandem pertinentibus non cancellatam non abolitam nec in aliqua sui parte viciatam in hec verba inspexisse

Universis Christi fidelibus ad quos præsens scriptum pervenerit. Rogerus Dei gracia etc. *Ut patet supra in ordinacione dicti Rogeri Episcopi usque ad sustinebunt.*

In premissorum autem testimonium et munimen presentem paginam sigillis nostris et sigillis Decani et Capituli Lichfeldie fecimus roborari saluo Coventrie et Lichfeldie Ecclesi jure pont. et parochiali. Acta apud Lichfeldiam in Crastino beati Thome Martiris. Anno Domini Millesimo CC^mo. quadragesimo octavo. December 30, 1248.

Nos igitur ordinacionem et appropriacionem antedictas canonicas et rite factas eas reputantes approbamus et pontificali auctoritate confirmamus. Saluis nobis et successoribus nostris et ecclesiis nostris juribus universis antedictis. In cnjus rei testimonium presentibus litteris sigillum nostrum fecimus apponi. Data apud Brewode in festo purificacionis beate Marie, anno gracie Millesimo CC^mo. Septuagesimo octavo Conserationis vero nostre vicesimo primo.—February 2, 1278-9.

### Appendix G.

The following arms, &c., were formerly in the windows of Wednesbury Church :—

1. A. a bend, cotised Gules.
2. A. a bend Gules, cotised Sa.
3. The same, impaling a fess between three fleur-de-lis.
4. Arg. a fess A. cotised Gules.
5. A. on a chief Or, three martlets Sa. impaling quarterly Ermine and Gules . . . in a bordure Az.
6. Arg. three covered cups Sa.
7. Sa. two lions passant Ar. crowned Or. (Heronvile.)
8. The same, within a bordure Or.
9. Or, two lions passant Az.
10. Arg. a fess between two chevrons Az. impaling Az. semée of fleurs-de-lis, a lion rampant Or. Over it is inscribed, " Jacobus Beaumont et Eliz. ux. ejus." But their arms are reversed.
11. A cross charged with 5 roses, impaling on a bend 3 stirrup irons. John Cumberford et Em. sa. feme. 1559.
12. On a bend 3 stags' heads impaling 3 chevronels. Georgius Stanley et Elianor, uxor.
13. Humfry Cumberford et Dor, ux. ejus. Arms : Cumberford and Beaumont as above.
14. John Babington et Johnna ux. Arms : Arg. nine torteauxes, a label of 3 points Az. impaling Beaumont.
15. The same arms. Hum. Babington et Elianor ux ejus.*

---

### Appendix H.—*Lectern.*

The lectern, as a component part of church furniture, may be traced to very early times—indeed, we find it mentioned as soon as churches were by law permitted to be erected. Its place was in front of the chancel, or at the

---

* Wyrley's Church Notes, 1597.

south side, and was surrounded by the seats appropriated to the choir. From it the Scriptures were accustomed to be read, and, in some instances, commented upon and explained by the officiating minister. As in other matters connected with the internal economy of the Church, the primitive Christians ever strove that all should be done "to edifying," so also with regard to the arrangement of the lectern choir the aim was not overlooked, the idea intended to be conveyed thereby being the manner in which the Saviour's birth was proclaimed to the shepherds. One angel alone declared the glad tidings—an innumerable multitude of the angelic host followed in exulting strains—so one authorised person read the Gospel of Peace, and was followed by the ravishing melody of the choristers, giving praise to God for all the things they had heard.

During the dark and degenerate ages of Popery, the lectern was retained as an article of ecclesiastical furniture. In an illuminated MS. of the tenth century, a desk is represented, in form corresponding with the modern lectern; and we find examples of the existence of such as early as the reign of King John. There is one of great antiquity in the Parish Church of Crowle, Worcestershire; another is preserved in the Abbey House, Wenlock, Salop; a third in the ancient church of Ramsay, Hants; and a fourth in Southwell Minster, Notts. They, for the most part, bear the figure of an eagle—symbolical at once of S. John the Evangelist, and of the angel commissioned to carry "the tidings of great joy" throughout the world.

At the period of the Reformation, lecterns were permitted to remain in their usual place in churches, as they were not considered, in any respect, to minister to superstition or idolatry, but were viewed rather as a useful, if not a necessary part of the Church's furniture; and it is a fact worth remarking, that of the lecterns existing at this time in England, by far the greater number were made *after* the Reformation—amongst many others those in York Minster; in S. Mary Redcliffe, Bristol; and in the Church of the Holy Trinity, Coventry. Previous to the Great Rebellion most of our parish churches possessed their lectern, nor were they regarded with suspicion until the fanatical and ignorant Roundheads termed them "remnants of Popery," and forthwith made havoc of them throughout the land, a spirit not altogether extinct in this our day.

That in the Old Church is one of the most ancient *wooden* lecterns in existence.

It may be as well to remark, that from the earliest times, lay-readers have been appointed, under certain restrictions, to read the lessons in the church, and thus to assist the minister—a custom still authorised by the Anglican Church.

----

### APPENDIX I.

The following account of the market held in Wednesbury is taken, by permission, from an unpublished history of the same :—

"It would appear from the Charter, granted to John Hoo, Esq., that two fairs are to be held in Wednesbury, viz. one on the 25th of April, and the other on the 23rd of July (old style,) for the buying and selling of all manner of cattle and beasts, and for all manner of goods, &c., that the market is to be held on the *Friday* in every week for the buying and selling of corn, flesh, fish, and all other provisions; that on those days, viz. on the fair and market days, reasonable tolls may be taken for all cattle, goods, &c. sold or exposed for sale in such fairs or markets, and that John

Hoo, Esq. was licensed to hold these two fairs in the year, and this Market on the Friday in every week, together with the court of pie-poudre, at the time and times of such fairs; and it would appear that on these fair and market days alone reasonable tolls, tollage, piccage, and stallage for cattle, goods, &c. sold or exposed for sale on such aforesaid days, may be received to the only and proper use and behoof of the said John Hoo, his heirs and assigns for ever. It would then seem that on no other days than the 25th of April and the 23d of July, on which days the fairs are held, and Friday in every week, on which the market is held, can tolls be legally taken by the representatives of the Lord of the Manor.

"To what extent the fairs and markets were carried on after the grant of the Charter we cannot ascertain; but certainly, from the evidence of some of the oldest inhabitants, there was little business transacted at them about the close of the last century. Friday could scarcely be distinguished from any other day in the week as a day of business; and for some time after, five or six stalls of meat constituted the whole of the market of Wednesbury. At that time one Joseph Harrison was town crier, keeper of the pin-fold, and beadle of the Parish Church, from which latter office he was dismissed in the year 1818. In what year Harrison began to receive tolls on the fair and market days cannot be ascertained, but certainly, at the time of his death, some fees were received by his son for the loan of stalls, and for stallage of goods sold or exposed for sale.

"About this time a few stalls might be seen in Wednesbury on the Saturday evening, and persons who brought goods for sale were accustomed to borrow stalls of Harrison, and pay him for the use of them. This led to an attempt to take tolls on the Saturday evening, and by lapse of time this impost has been claimed as a matter of right; and tolls are now demanded as on the regular market day. On the death of Harrison, which took place in 1822, Peter Ellis was appointed to the vacant office. At this time no rent was received by the Lords of the Manor, and Ellis was appointed on the same terms and conditions as his predecessors, viz. ' without paying any acknowledgment in the form of rent.' This appointment, however, was very soon cancelled. Joseph Harrison, the son of the old beadle, at the suggestion of one Michael Toney, obtained an interview with some one in authority, and by offering the stewards a small annual payment (about £10 per annum), induced them to place him in his late father's office. At the wake, the *constable* had, for many years past, been in the habit of collecting small gratuities from some booth and show-

men, and paying them over to the treasurer of the Sunday School. Soon
after Harrison's appointment, he laid claim to these gratuities, and in order
to settle the dispute, a copy of the original Charter was obtained in 1826
by Mr. Joseph Dawes, the churchwarden, who caused it to be printed·
This at once decided the matter, so that Harrison forthwith resigned his
claim, and confined his collections at the wake time to those persons for
whose accommodation he provided stalls.    Harrison died in the month of
March, 1840, and was succeeded by Thomas Tibbets, who had for many
years been parish constable.   The annual rent was now advanced to the
sum of £20 per annum.    Tibbets, when constable, had for some time
collected the gratuities from the booth and showmen, and at the wake,
and paid them over to the treasurer of the Schools:  this he did both before and after he was appointed collector of the tolls, but being excluded
from the office of constable, he ceased to pay any more.    In 1845 Tibbets
paid the sum of £5, and with this year the custom ceased.

" Previous to the time of the wake, in the year 1848, it was determined
not to allow the large booths to be erected in the Market Place, and
orders were given to the police to that effect.   On the Monday morning,
however, in the wake week, a person of the name of Douglas, master of a
company of strolling players, came into the town and began to prepare to
erect his booth in the most conspicuous part of the Market Place.   When
told by the Superintendent of the Police that he would not be allowed to
proceed, he replied, " Oh! but I have taken the ground a month ago, and
paid £5 for the use of it."    Thus, the very Market Place was let for an
illegal purpose, the Charter only authorising toll to be taken for goods and
merchandise exposed for sale on market and fair days.   Douglas was told that
Tibbets (with whom he had agreed for the ground) had  no right to let it
to any one, much  less to a gang of players.    After some demur, however,
the booth was suffered to be erected, but subsequently Douglas summoned
Tibbets for obtaining money under false pretences.    The following is a
copy of the summons :—

*County of Stafford.—To the Constable of the Parish of Wednesbury, in the
said County, and to all other Constables and Peace Officers for the said
County.*

These are, in Her Majesty's name, to require you, upon sight hereof, to
summon Thomas Tibbets, collector of tolls of the parish of Wednesbury,
in the  said county, personally to  appear before such of Her Majesty's

Justices of the Peace for the said county of Stafford, as shall be assembled
at the Public Office, in Wednesbury, in the said county of Stafford, on the
12th day of September, 1848, at ten o'clock in the forenoon, to answer the
complaint of John Douglas, of the parish of Wednesbury, in the said
county of Stafford, travelling player, for that he, the said Thomas Tibbets,
did, on the 4th day of August, 1848, at the parish of Wednesbury, in the
said county of Stafford, knowingly, unlawfully, and designedly, by false
pretences then and there made by him, that is to say, by pretending that
as collector of the tolls of the Market at Wednesbury aforesaid, he had the
right of permitting the said John Douglas to occupy a part of the Market
Place, at Wednesbury aforesaid, on certain days not being the days on
which a market is usually held at Wednesbury aforesaid, obtain from the
said John Douglas certain monies, to wit, the sum of five pounds of the
monies of the said John Douglas, with intent then and there to cheat
and defraud the said John Douglas of the same, contrary to the statute in
such case made and provided. Herein fail not. Given under my hand
and seal, the 11th day of September, 1848. I. CLARKSON.—*Summon to
give evidence.*

"The case was heard before the Rev. I. Clarkson, John Leigh, Esq.,
Stipendiary Magistrate, and P. Williams, Esq., Sept. 19, 1848. Mr.
Holland, attorney, West Bromwich, appeared for the plaintiff, and Mr.
Bolton, attorney, Wolverhampton, for the defendant.

"Mr. Holland opened the proceedings by stating very briefly that the
defendant was charged with having taken the sum of £5, as collector of
of the fair and market tolls, at a time when he had no right to do so;
that he knew that his right to the tolls did not extend beyond the fair
and market days; and that he practised deceit upon the plaintiff, and
thus defrauded him of £5.

"John Douglas examined.—I am master of a company of players.
About a month ago I made application to Tibbets for land in the Market-
place whereon to erect my booth for the wake. Tibbets said I might
have the land for £5. I understood him to say that he had the right of
letting it, and I treated with him under that impression. We walked over
the land, and I agreed to pay his demand. I should not have paid him
if I had not believed he was entitled to it. He represented himself as
entitled to it. I was to erect on Monday.

"Cross-examined.—He told me he had received it for years from Holloway. I was to have five days, and one was Friday. It was one contract

for the whole time. I would not have given £5 for one day. We had no talk about any division of the money. He treated with me openly. I had no reason to suspect he was defrauding me.

"Mrs. Douglas.—I received some money from my husband about a month ago, and I came to Wednesbury and paid Tibbets £5 for the standing for the wake. I asked him to give me a receipt for it. He refused, but said it would be all right—we should either have the standing, or he would return the money.

"John Yardley.—I have lived in Wednesbury all my life. There are two fairs in the year, and a market every week on the Friday. There is a wake in the beginning of September. I was constable fourteen or fifteen years. Joseph Harrison was collector of the tolls on the fair and market days. I received the gratuities for the booths and shows, and paid them to the treasurer of the Sunday Schools. Harrison received no tolls at the wake, except for fees for the loan of his own stalls.

"Samuel Harrison.—I am about thirty-three years old. I often assisted my father to collect the tolls on the fair days and market days; and during his illness, I collected them for him, and for my mother a short time after his death. We did not collect any tolls at the wake, except from those to whom we lent stalls. The constable collected some money from those who had booths and shows, and paid it to the schools

"Mr. Joseph Smith.—1 remember Mr. Tibbets being constable. At the time of the wake, he used to come and tell me what he had received, and he paid it to the treasurer of the schools. In 1845, Tibbits had received money—I believe about £8—and he hesitated about giving it up to the schools. After some altercation, he agreed to pay £5. I was churchwarden, and a member of the Board of Surveyors. The Board of Surveyors claimed the money for the schools.

"Mr. Joseph Dawes.—I am constable for the Leet at the present time. I have given no authority to Tibbets to collect any gratuities. I went round last year and the year before to collect gratuities, but I was told Tibbets had been before me, and received the money. I suppose he kept it for his own use.

"Mr. Bolton argued, that if Tibbets had done wrong in taking this £5, the surveyors had been equally guilty in collecting or claiming gratuities. Suppose Tibbets had no right to receive this money from Douglas, still it must be regarded only as a mistake. There is no proof that he has knowingly and fraudulently obtained it. He considered he had, as collector of the tolls, a right to demand this fee ; and I submit that, where even a supposed right is maintained, there can be no intentional and designed fraud. I call no witnesses.

" Mr. Leigh doubted whether Tibbets had intentionally defrauded Douglas. He contends that he supposed he had a right to this fee ; but the evidence of custom is decidedly against him. He may be indicted at the sessions; but would not a jury consider that he acted under a mistake ? Clearly his right to the tolls was confined to the fair and market days, as was evident both from the Charter and from custom; and any future attempt to obtain what did not belong to him after this warning must tell against him. We might bind him over to appear, on notice, to answer any indictment that may be preferred against him ; but I think the best course is to dismiss the present charge, and leave the parties concerned to proceed against him, if they think proper, at the next sessions.

" The Magistrates were unanimous in their opinion that the defendant had no right to tolls, except on the fair and market days, and though they dismissed the present case because there did not appear from the evidence so much guilty knowledge as to justify a committal for a misdemeanour, yet they hesitated not to declare that no evidence had been elicited, either from custom or from the charter, to give the defendant the slightest pretext for claiming the money he had received.

" For many years a custom prevailed in Wednesbury of ' *Walking the Fair.*' The ceremonies connected with it were conducted in the following manner :—On the morning of the fair, Harrison, the beadle, appeared in the Market Place, dressed for the occasion, and bearing, as badges of his office, a bell, a long pike, &c. To him assembled a number of the principal inhabitants of the parish, often with a band of music. They then marched in procession, headed by the beadle, through different parts of the town, called at the ' Elephant and Castle,' in the ' High Bullen,' then kept by one Nash, drank two tankards of ale, and then returned into the Market Place, where they quenched their thirst again with the same kind of beverage. After this they dined together at one of the public houses. The expenses incurred in this 'walking the fair' were defrayed by the parish funds.

" In the centre of the Market Place formerly stood an unsightly building, commonly called the ' *Cross.*' It was built upon pillars and arches, and consisted of two upper rooms, to which there was an entrance,

W

at the north end, by an uncouth flight of steps. In these rooms a number of children were taught, the school being supported by the inhabitants. Formerly eight boys were clothed and educated by funds raised by yearly collections in the Parish Church; upon one of these occasions the celebrated William Romaine, Rector of S. Ann's, Blackfriars, preached the sermons. Here, too, commissioners held their court of requests; magistrates sat to administer justice; and, on the top of the steps, tied to the door posts, many a culprit has been flogged by the beadle. Under the rooms, and within the arches, was a receptacle for all kinds of filth and dirt, and many a scene of vice and impurity has been witnessed there. This place had at last become so great a nuisance to the town that it was determined to take it down, especially as its dilapidated state rendered it dangerous to all passers by. Frequent applications were made to the Stewards of the Lords of the Manor to repair and improve it, but all applications were refused, until about thirty years ago, when, upon the request being repeated, Mr. Robins, one of the agents, replied, 'the parish might do what they liked with it, the Lords of the Manor would not repair it.' In the year 1824 some of the parishioners determined to pull it down, and the constable, Mr. John Yardley, by their direction took down the building, sold the old materials, and with the proceeds of that memorable sale repaired the parish walls. Thus ended the celebrated 'Wednesbury Cross.'"

---

*Augmentation Office Records.—Enrolments of Leases, fifth Elizabeth, Roll 21, No. 3.*

*Staffordia.*—Regina omnibus ad quos &c. salutem Cum tenementum et unum parvum croftum pasture eidem tenemento pertinens scituata jacencia et existencia in Weddisburye et Tipton, in Comitatu nostro Staffordie, dimissa inter alia pro annuali redditu sexdecim solidorum non solum antiquo tempore concelata fuerunt a nobis et progenitoribus nostris sed eciam ad presens magnopere in ruina et decasu existencia ut eadem absque grandibus sumptibus et oneribus reparare et manutenere quam non valeant Iamque pro eo quod dilectus nobis Robertus Cawdwell super se assumere vult tam reparacionem eorumdem sumptibus suis propriis et expensis reparare et manutenere quam annuatim respondere nobis heredibus et successoribus nostris predictum redditum sexdecim solidorum ut

supra specificatum. Sciatis igitur quod nos tam in consideracione predicta
quam pro fine quatuor librarum quindecim solidorum et quator denariorum
legalis monete Anglie ad receptam Scaccarii nostri ad usum nostrum per
predictum Robertum Cawdwell solutorum de avisamento Thesaurarii nostri
Anglie Cancellarii et Subthesaurarii Scaccarii nostri tradidimus concessimus et ad firmam dimisimus ac per presentes tradimus concedimus et ad
firmam dimittimus prefato Roberto Cawdwell omnes illas quinque crofta
pasture cum pertinenciis jacentes et existentes in Tipton modo vel nuper
in tenuris sive occupacionibus Georgii Hopkis et Ricardi Hopkis ac eciam
totum illud tenementum nostrum in Weddisburye cum pertinenciis ac
unum parvum croftum pasture nostrum eidem pertinentem jacentem in
Tipton modo vel nuper in tenura sive occupacione Willielmi Sudley Que
omnia et singula premissa scituantur jacencia et existencia in Weddisburye
et Tipton predictis in predicto Comitatu Staffordie ac nuper parcella
servicii beate Marie in ecclesia de Weddisburye vocati "our Lady's Service"
quondam spectabant et pertinebant ac parcella possessionum inde quondam existebant ac omnia et singula domos edificia structuras horrea
stabula columbaria hortos pomaria gardina terras prata pascua pasturas
communias ac omnia alia proficua commoditates advantagia emolumenta
et hereditamenta nostra quecumque cum eorum pertinenciis universis
premissis sive eorum alicui quoquo modo spectantibus vel pertinentibus
Exceptis tamen semper et nobis heredibus et successoribus nostris omnino
reservatis omnibus grossis arboribus boscis subboscis mineris et quarreris
premissorum. Habendum et tenendum omnia et singula premissa superius
expressa et specificata cum eorum pertinenciis universis prefato Roberto
Cawdwell executoribus et assignatis suis a festo Annunciacionis Beate
Marie Virginis ultimo preterito usque ad finem termini et per terminum
viginti et unius annorum ex tunc proximo sequencium et plenarie com.
plendorum Reddendo inde annuatim nobis heredibus et successoribus
nostris quadraginta septem solidos et octo denarios videlicet de et pro
predictis quinque croftis pasture cum pertinenciis in Tipton ut prefertur
existentibus triginta unum solidos et octo denarios Ac de et pro predicto
tenemento et parva crofto pasture in Weddnisburye et Tipton ut prefertur
existentibus sexdecim solidos legalis monete Anglie ad festa Sancti
Michaelis Archangeli et Annunciacionis Beate Marie Virginis ad receptam Scaccarii nostri seu ad manus Ballivorum vel Receptorum premissorum pro tempore existente per equales porciones solvendos durante

termino predicto Et predictus Robertus Cawdwell executores et assignati
sui omnia domos et edificia ac omnes alias necessarias reparaciones premissorum in omnibus et per omnia de tempore in tempus tociens quo-
ciens necesse et oportum fuerit sumptibus suis propriis et expensis bene
et sufficienter reparabunt supportabunt sustinebunt escurabunt purga-
bunt et manutenebunt durante termino predicto ac premissa sufficienter reparata et manutenta in fine termini predicti dimittent Et volumus
ac per presentes concedimus prefato Roberto Cawdwell executoribus et
assignatis suis quod bene licebit eis de tempore in tempus capere per-
cipere et habere de in et super premissis crescentem competentem et
sufficientem housebote hedgebote fierbote ploughbote et cartebote ibidem
et non alibi annuatim expendendum et occupandum durante termino
predicto Et quod habeant maeremium in boscis et terris premissorum
crescens ad et versus reparacionem domorum et edificiorum premissorum
per assignacionem et supervisionem Seneschi seu Subseneschi aut
aliorum officiariorum nostrorum heredum et successorum nostrorum
ibidem pro tempore existente durante termino predicto Proviso semper
quod si contigerit predictos separales redditus aut eorum aliquem a retro
fore non solutos in parte vel in toto per spacium quadraginta dierum
post aliquod festum festorum predictorum quout prefertur solvi debeant
durante termino predicto quod tunc et deinceps hæc presens dimissio et
concessio vacua sit ac pro nullo habeatur aliquo in presentibus in con-
trarium inde non obstante aliquo statuto &c.   In cujus rei &c. Teste
&c. apud Westmonasterium sexto die Julii anno Regni nostri quinto.

————

*Wednesbray to wit.—At a Court of Humphrey Comberford, Esquire, there
holden on Sunday, the Nineteenth Day of November, in the Fourth
Year of the Reign of Edward the Sixth, by the Grace of God of
England, France, and Ireland, King, Defender of the Faith, and on
Earth of the Church of England and Ireland Supreme Head, it is thus
enrolled :—*

At this Court came Richard Field, and surrendered into the hands of
the Lord, according to the custom of the Manor, One Croft, called
Sillimor's Hall, near Dymock's Green, to the use and behoof of Edward
Nyghtingalle, his heirs and assigns for ever:   And whereupon here, at

this same Court, came the said Edward Nyghtyngalle in his own proper person, and took of the Lord the Croft aforesaid, with the Appurtenances, to hold to him and his heirs according to the custom of the Manor, by the services therefore formerly due and accustomed : To whom the Lord by his Steward granted seisin thereof : And the said Edward gives to the Lord, for a Fine, 6s. 8d., and does fealty to the Lord, and is admitted Tenant thereof : In witness whereof to this present Copy I have put my Seal, the Day and Year above mentioned.

Examined by me, RICHARD CATHERALL,

Deputy Steward there.

## Parish Church Schools.

ALTHOUGH the schools in connection with the Parish Church ought, on every account, to take precedence of the others ; yet, by an inadvertent omission, they come to be mentioned last. The first part was built in 1829, by a grant from the Lichfield Diocesan Society, aided by local subscriptions, together amounting to £400. The second part was added in 1843, and the necessary funds raised as follows :—

|  | £ | s. | d. |
|---|---|---|---|
| Grants from the Lords of the Treasury . | 180 | 0 | 0 |
| National Society  .  .  .  .  . | 105 | 0 | 0 |
| Lichfield Diocesan Society  .  .  . | 30 | 0 | 0 |
|  | 315 | 0 | 0 |
| Subscriptions  .  .  -  .  .  . | 269 | 7 | 6 |
|  | £584 | 7 | 6 |

The site for both schools was given by the late Sir E. D. Scott, Bart., and E. T. Foley, Esq.

The play ground was added in 1852, the land being given by Sir E. D. Scott, Bart., and the Lady Emily Foley.

The following is the total cost of these schools :—

|  | £ | s. | d. |
|---|---|---|---|
| First erection | 400 | 0 | 0 |
| Second ditto | 584 | 7 | 6 |
| Enclosing and levelling play ground (raised by local subscription) | 106 | 0 | 0 |
|  | £1090 | 7 | 6 |

These schools have accommodation for 180 girls, and about 200 boys.

# Pedigrees.

¦ Hen. II. or Step

¦ 40 Hen. III.⹀

Richard Co

ᵽry, eldest daught

Sollinghull.⹀Ma

John, Lord of

d.⹀Johanna.

⹀nna.        Willia

f Shitlehanger.

hter of John Coope

lla, daughter of  .
ishop Hatfield, cou

daughter        Hu
hn Breton,
ᶥamworth.

1598.        Elizabeth

Buried at⹀Mary

f Edward        Rob
n.

f Salop.        Anne,

ᵽr Anne.

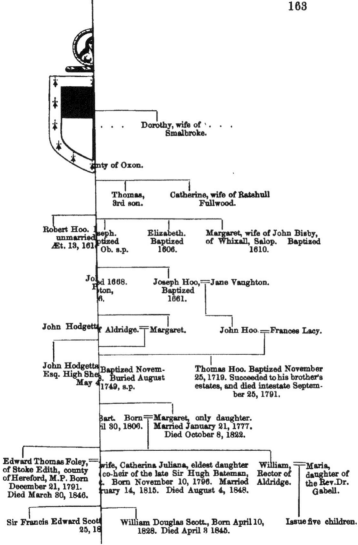

. . . Dorothy, wife of ʹ. . . . Smalbroke.

ʹ......nty of Oxon.

Thomas, 3rd son.　　Catherine, wife of Ratshull Fullwood.

Robert Hoo. unmarried Æt. 13, 161...　Joseph. ...ptized ...Ob. s.p.　　Elizabeth. Baptized 1606.　　Margaret, wife of John Bisby, of Whixall, Salop. Baptized 1610.

Jo...d 1668. ...ton, ...6.　　Joseph Hoo, = Jane Vaughton. Baptized 1661.

John Hodgetts ... Aldridge. = Margaret.　　John Hoo. = Frances Lacy.

John Hodgetts Esq. High She... May 4...　...Baptized Novem-...3. Buried August 1749, s.p.　　Thomas Hoo. Baptized November 25, 1719. Succeeded to his brother's estates, and died intestate September 25, 1791.

...art. Born = Margaret, only daughter. ...il 30, 1806. Married January 21, 1777. Died October 8, 1822.

Edward Thomas Foley, = wife, Catherina Juliana, eldest daughter of Stoke Edith, county co-heir of the late Sir Hugh Bateman, of Hereford, M.P. Born ... Born November 10, 1796. Married December 21, 1791. ...uary 14, 1815. Died August 4, 1848. Died March 30, 1846.　　William, = Maria, Rector of daughter of Aldridge. the Rev. Dr. Gabell.

Sir Francis Edward Scott ... 25, 18...　　William Douglas Scott., Born April 10, 1828. Died April 3 1845.　　Issue five children.

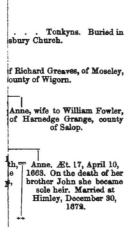

. . . Tonkyns. Buried in
sbury Church.

f Richard Greaves, of Moseley,
ounty of Wigorn.

Anne, wife to William Fowler,
of Harnedge Grange, county
of Salop.

h, ⚭ Anne. Æt. 17, April 10,
e | 1663. On the death of her
r, | brother John she became
| sole heir. Married at
| Himley, December 30,
| 1672.

.   daughter of  .   .   .   Nash, of Lye
Court, in the county of Hereford.

r of Thomas Andrews, of  .   .   .   county
       of Salop.

county of Gloucester, Esq. by Blanch, his
Witton, county of Salop.

o George        3rd Sarah.  Married Robert
in the          Crump, 2nd son of Thomas
e, in the       Crump, of Drayton, county
                   of Hereford.

o 1683.         2nd, Margaret.  Aged 0 months
                      anno 1683.

pkns, of t

an. Died

m Court, county of Surrey, Gent.  Liv. 1622.

ght, wife
nit, Lor esson,
Shdied which
h Octob of
St. ither ber 7,
enh Stre 1691 ;

Jane, wife of John
Cave, Horsepool
Grange, county of
Leicester, Esq.

Anne, wife of Matthew
Babington, of Temple
Rochley, county of
Leicester, Esq.

rd  Ma
ns,
n.

Ha nas Hopkins, youngest
Da 1686, Secretary to Lord
c nderland; Steward of
eic oventry, and a Com-
sioner of Salt Duties.

Elizabeth.
Liv. 1650.
Ob. before
1672.

Sarah, wife of Sir
John Goodrick, of
Ribston, county of
York, Bart..  He
died December 10,
1705.

Suffk716
d at Mic
y.

d February 28, 1725.

Elizabeth.
Liv. 1672.

Mary.  Liv. 1691.  A minor 1706.
Unmarried 1709.

, an 5.
he ci L
Novel,

House, county of Wilts, M.P., LL.D.,⟞Anne. Born in St. James's Place.
1770.  Buried at Box, county of Wilts,│Married in 1751, at Messenden,
, 1769; proved December 31. 1770.   │county of Bucks.  Liv. 1800.

The son and grandson both took the name of Hopkins.

lliam Rose, of

Anne, daug William and Sarah (twins.) Born 1698, at Daventry.

Anne, den, of Birmingham, county of Warwick; Patron of
ter, county of Essex. Born December 3, 1717, at
ry. Died March 6, 1806. Buried at Wednesbury.

Clare Hall, Ca n Rose Holden, eldest son and heir. Married June,
f Parliament, ary, daughter of William Tovey, of Erdington, county
4, at Whilton. of Stafford.

Rose, B.D.; er 19, 1799.
d Tutor of uary 22, 1783. Buried April 24, 1787, at Daventry.
ege, Oxford; 1 16, 1784.
His Majesty's 3, 1787.
t Whitehall. Buried November 30, 1789, at Daventry.
20, and bap- y 23, 1793, at Daventry.
e 19, 1788. as buried the 18th of May, 1797, at Daventry.

Conway Lucas Hyla Holden Rose. Born November 4, 1811, at
Greenwich, county of Kent.

y, in the county o

776, aged about

=Mary, Daught yla Holden. Died at Bath about 1766. Buried at Wednesbury. Married and had issue.

ate of Summer H ed December 9, 1829, aged        Rev. William Lucas Holden, afterwards
gham. Died Janu                                 Rev. William Lucas Rose.

Hyla Hol an Elizabeth.   Rev. Henry Augustus Holden,  Mary, daughter of Hyda
county of gust 27, 1792.  of Daventry, county of North-  Holden, of Wednesbury
3rd sur infant. Buried    hampton; M.A. of Worcester    Forge, county of Stafford.
Novembe pminster.         College, Oxford; 6th, but 4th  Married September 9,
December                  surviving son. Born Decem-     1813, at Wednesbury.
                          ber 27, 1784. Baptized at S.
                          George the Martyr's, London.

Elizabeth,      une   Mary Tovey. Born March 13,    George Hyla    Eleanor D'Ouchy.
ter of John     d at  1820. Baptized at S. Martin's,  Holden. Born   Born September
am, of the East ing-  Birmingham. Married Novem-     November 23,   24, 1833, at Ouchy,
npany's service. pril  ber 22, 1849, at S. Giles's,   1827. Baptized  in Switzerland, and
May 14, 1836, at od   Middlesex, Hyda Ashton         at Warrington.  baptized
s, county of          Holden, of Edgbaston, county   Died unmarried  at Brighton.
orcester.             of Warwick.

in Sydney, Marc 5,   Reuben Thomas. Born January    Oswald Maugin. Born December
following.   Buri    5, and died January 8, 1842.              6, 1843.
matta.               Buried at Whittington.

# Index.

—

## PLATES OF ARMS.

| No. 1.—Heronville | No. 2.—Hoo | No. 3.—Parkes |
|---|---|---|
| Leventhorp | Scott | Hopkins |
| Comberford | Paget | St. Paul |
| Beaumont | Foley | Rose |
| Comberford | Wednesbury | Holden |

Wolverhampton: W. PARKE, Printer, High Street.

Lightning Source UK Ltd.
Milton Keynes UK
UKHW020825270223
417728UK00007B/694